Inside my Head

Messages from a Medium

Jennie Ogilvie

ISBN 978-1-7387414-0-3 (Paperback)

ISBN 978-1-7387414-1-0 (E-book)

Dedicated to all of my life lessons and experiences thus far. Here is to all of the YES in my life. Thank you.

Foreword

Pulling the Weeds of My Soul Garden

Foreword by author and podcaster Dana Goldstein

Before I even met Jennie, I felt compelled to speak to her. I sometimes give credence to my "woo" side and listen when my instincts are screaming at me. Immediately after watching a Facebook video of Jennie, I looked her up and called her.

"I'm not sure why I feel this way," I told her, "but we need to work together."

My initial thought when I met Jennie was that she would be fantastic in front of the camera. Her energy was infectious and I knew I wanted to capture that through video. In all my years as a videographer, I can count on one hand those people who naturally shine in front of the lens. That conversation planted the seed for a pilot—an episode that Jennie could use as the first for a potential series (and would later be squashed by the COVID pandemic). I trailed her for a weekend with three cameras filming her live shows, our conversations in her car, formal interviews in her hotel room, and post-reading wrap-ups. The footage was astounding, and it was over these three days that I learned three things:

1. Jennie is the real deal. The details she provides during readings are astonishing, not just to the person being read, but to everyone in the audience, including me.
2. I am an empath, and as such, I feel the emotions of others just as much as I feel Jennie's vibrant energy.
3. Searching for answers, or a way to assuage our grief, is a universal experience that supersedes race, religion, or social status.

But when I first met Jennie, I was seriously uncomfortable. Here is a woman—a lesbian who says she talks to dead people—who is living large. She doesn't hold back what she's feeling or thinking. Her laugh is infectious, as is her need to swear at every turn. She is always making a point and will repeat a question, firing it back at you until you squirm.

Every single one of her shows sells out and people follow her everywhere, emulating the fandom of the

Grateful Dead. Before meeting Jennie, I didn't believe in mediums, having been exposed more than once to someone who was clearly a fraud looking to make a buck. But over and over again, I saw Jennie change people's minds. A visibly skeptical woman in her early 70s nearly choked on her tea when Jennie brought up the brand new fancy bra and underwear the woman had recently purchased. Another woman gripped the sides of her chair so tight when Jennie turned to her and said, "You know, you *should* go to Paris." How can anyone explain how Jennie knew the woman had been planning a trip with her husband, but when he passed, the dream swirled away like broken leaves in the wind?

After 24 hours with Jennie, a shift happened within me. I was being pulled to the side where I could suspend disbelief and buy into this thing called mediumship. Over the course of a single day, I watched her stun people over and over with details she shouldn't know. We were having a casual conversation as we drove to the first show of the weekend when she dropped a zinger, asking me, "What is your legacy?"

I didn't have an answer, and under her scrutiny, I was uneasy about that fact. She gave me the weekend to think about it.

There were a lot of firsts for me over those three days in May. It was the first time I had ever seen a medium live in action. It was the first time I was wholly attached to my cameras, always ready to start filming should something incredible happen (which it did) or should Jennie have an inspiration (which she did, shortly after 5 a.m.). For the first time in my adult life, I considered taking a bath in a hotel room, so great was the need to soak away the emotion of the day.

The weekend was transformative for me. I was able to pull the weeds from my soul garden, that place where joy is unfiltered and complete. I opened my mind. I let my emotions run wild. Even though I was working, I was able to do some deep work, letting my brain churn in the background to figure out what my legacy was in the stories I tell—my own and those of others.

After the weekend was through, Jennie let me borrow her car to head home. She was catching a ride with someone else, so I had two and a half hours on my own to process that this person who barely knew me had blindly handed me the keys. A level of trust like that has to be earned, I thought. But Jennie *knows* shit. She knew I was going to drive that car with the utmost caution and care. She knew I was going to get home safely. And she knew that the weekend had made space for the flowers to grow in my soul garden. For that, I am always grateful.

This Book Is Your Chicken Soup

Think of this book as that package of chicken soup you have buried in your pantry. It's been there forever, abandoned since the last time you were sick or had a craving. You might have even had a kid since you bought it. When you bought it, the expiry date was long into the future. And with each new item you put in the pantry, the package got pushed back farther and farther, until you forgot it was there. But when you need it, you'll remember it's there.

You've picked up this book because something inside said you needed it. This book is your chicken soup. It's easy to follow the instructions and in three to five minutes, you'll have a cupful of goodness.

Stick with me for the ride. My thoughts are random, and this book is a reflection of that. Some thoughts are deep and will make you think, and some will make you wonder if I'm okay (I am, for the most part). This book can be read in order, all at once, or at your leisure. If you feel guided to open the book randomly, that works too. It might be the universe delivering a message you need, or it might be Spirit guiding you.

However you turn the pages, by the end of this book you'll have some really great, no-bullshit perspectives that may help you find a way to heal, give you something to laugh about, or reduce you to tears. I've taken the lessons I've learned over the years—some because of my own stupid moves, others from Spirit—and tried to break down the mountains into mud puddles.

Laugh. Cry. Repeat.

Here we go.

Swing, You Crazy Monkey

When we're young, if we're fortunate, fear and death are completely foreign to us. We swing from the monkey bars, never considering we'll fall. We love with our whole hearts, never giving a second thought to the idea that the people around us won't be there forever. Children don't understand that life has a finality and because of that, they live life to the fullest. Somewhere down the line, death becomes something we fear. Most people are overwhelmed by death. I get it. It's an ending, a loss, and it's wrapped in heartbreak.

Well, I'm not most people. I am inspired by death, and not just because Spirit is whispering in my ear. While you're here on this Earth, you get to command the narrative and tell the story of your life, your way. Death is just the period at the end of your whole existence.

Death is the final mark.

You know it's coming, so why not make the most of the life you have? Leave a legacy of love, of laughter, of generosity.

Do your best to go to the grave without leaving behind bitterness and anger.

Fix your shit.

Apologize for your asshattery.

Let your loved ones smile when they think of you,

not spit on your Facebook profile. Teach the people you love what it feels like to be loved by you.

Recall some of that magic of childhood and be the best you can be. Remember what it was like to never have a doubt about who you are and what you can do. Kids are forever learning something new. Every day is an opportunity to grow. If someone tells you not to pursue your dream, or has put the bug in your ear that you can't, remember your child voice: "I can do it!" At five, you could tie your laces. At 10, you could load and empty the dishwasher without breaking a single plate. At 20, you saw the world as your oyster.

Live with purpose because death is coming for all of us.

Make your life matter by the time you get to the period at the end. Death shows up to remind you to live, to not shit your pants, to never give up.

Swing wildly my monkeys.

Losing the Popularity Contest

This book is filled with lessons for living by examining what happens when someone close to us has died. It won't be gruesome, but sometimes it will be uncomfortable. I want to challenge you to think about how you are living your life.

Are you doing the best you can or is that a lie you tell yourself? Are you immobilized by grief and regret? You don't need me or Spirit to tell you how badly you are messing up this one shot at a fulfilling life.

Listen, questioning what you're doing with your life is inevitable in the wake of someone's death. That's part of being human. It's how we move forward from there that matters. Stand in your strength. Apologize to those you have hurt. Envision the legacy you want to leave behind.

If nothing else, consider this book a smack to the side of your head. It's your wake-up call before you never wake up again. *Live your damn life.* That's how you win your crown.

This book is as much about you as it is about me. I started out writing a plain old memoir, but it wasn't working for me. Believe it or not, I like to keep some things very private. That's kind of funny given what I do for a living. I poke around in the Spirit world and get details about people.

Scratch that.

Spirit pokes around in my head and shows me things I shouldn't know about the people I read for. Sometimes, Spirit shows me things I'm embarrassed to share and that says a lot for a lesbian who stands in front of a room of strangers, cursing and telling people she talks to the dead.

Even though I make people laugh and cry and connect, I am judged every time I step in front of a crowd for a live reading. They are looking at how I stand, how I tend to rub my hands alongside my breasts (sexy, I know) when I am channelling Spirit. They look at my shoes, my glasses, and my ass as I pace the stage, plucking symbols out of my brain and making sense of them for someone in the audience.

People either like me or they don't. They either believe or they don't. I'm not going to spend energy changing someone's opinion. That's not my job. It's not Spirit's job either. Spirit cannot tell you if you should take that new job or move or marry the person who asked you. We're not in the business of fixing your life. Only you can do that.

Spirit and I are just here to connect you with the messages someone wants you to hear. It's up to you to decide to make the changes.

What Do I See

People ask me all the time what I see when I am channelling. Over the years, I've struggled to explain this. In the early days, I probably said something like, "I can see energy flowing like waves in the ocean," or "I see pieces of string that are connected to Spirit and I pull them like an amusement park game."

It was vague, because I couldn't yet put what I saw into words. I've now been doing this long enough that I can explain it a bit better.

It's like this: When we both look up into the sky, we can see clouds. You might see shapes, or dark edges indicating a storm is coming. I see that cloud too, but inside that cloud, I see movement. In that movement, I see a source. Within that source, I see an awareness. And in that awareness, I see my journey with you.

I don't see the exact same cloud every time. What I see changes, and it's different for every person I read. No one's energy is exactly the same.

I'm Not Fine

What if the next time someone asked you how you were, you said, "I'm not fine?"

Our trigger response is usually, "I'm fine, thank you." Why do we answer that way? Because nobody wants to deal with your shit, not even you.

It's an interesting contrast to what really happens. Humans love to bitch and moan loudly about the negative stuff we pick up on from others before we talk about the good stuff.

When it comes to our own crap, we're "fine," even when we're hurting inside, grieving and guilt-ridden. Why is it so hard to tell someone that we're not fine? It's not up to you to manage how someone else will respond if you answer "I'm actually a fucking mess right now." Who knows what could happen? You might make a deeper connection with another person who is also in pain or who can help or who will just listen to you for a minute.

What I find fascinating is how easily we grieve or mourn when someone famous dies. We openly share our loss on social media, despite the fact that this is not someone we know personally. Still, we are deeply connected to the experiences that celebrity gave us. When a celebrity dies, especially if they were part of our teenage development, two things are happening:

1. You are staring your own mortality in the face.
2. You are reminded (whether you acknowledge this or not) of how simple things were before you had adult responsibilities.

We all have shitty days. When someone famous dies, it gives us a chance to reflect and to process. The beauty of celebrity status is that their stories live on forever in books, movies, and across the internet. Your favourites will still be there when you need them. You will still stop scrolling Netflix when you come across your favourite comfort movie.

Death is not always bad news. For some, it will be a negative experience, but for most of us, it's our chance to grieve and eventually heal so we can move on. For some, it will take a long time to be fine. When people ask you if you are okay, especially after you've lost someone, it's *fine* to admit that you're not. It's also *fine* to acknowledge that you are.

When someone passes, we are told to celebrate the good things, focus on the happy memories. Why the hell can't we do that every day? Life is a triumph over death, my friend. So for every day that you wake up—fine or not—you should share the shit out of life.

The Brightest Star

Ask any medium and they'll tell you they knew from a young age that they were different from other kids. Like most little girls, I had my Barbie dolls and I played house. I also liked playing marbles and beating up boys—at least until the sixth grade when they grew bigger and stronger than me.

And like other children, I was also fond of asking questions. So *many questions*. The difference was, I didn't see things the same way as everyone else and I certainly didn't believe grown-ups when they told me how I should see things.

The embarrassment this caused my family became apparent when my Grampy died when I was five years old. It was the late '70s, when free love and free spirit was still a thing. At least, on TV it was. In my small town, where houses were spread far apart but the people were closer than your own asshole, there was no room for free will or for a little girl who questioned *everything*.

When Grampy died, all the kids were told he went to the brightest star in the sky, because that's where heaven was. The other two kids in my family, cousins who were the same age as me, ran outside at night looking up for the place where Grampy might be.

"Is that really heaven?" I asked. "How do we know that for sure?"

The adults around me answered me the way people typically do when they don't know what to say. They tried to silence me.

"Why do you ask so many questions? Heaven *is* the biggest star in the sky. Why can't you just accept that?"

"Then why aren't *you* out there looking at it if it's so important?"

That's the kind of kid I was. I always asked a million questions and doubted every answer. I was annoying to most, but I never thought my questions were really that out of line.

Even then, as a child, Spirit was whispering in my ear, pushing me in a different direction from everyone else. I was aware of a different level of existence, but I wasn't able to put a name to what I felt and heard. I never thought I was the weird one; I thought it was strange that other people couldn't see or hear what I did. I still feel that way sometimes.

Before I knew I had a connection to Spirit, I was pulled into strong connections with other people. I lacked the vocabulary to explain it, and family, friends, or teachers would shake their heads in wonder when I showed up on their doorstep, again. I *needed* to be at their place all the time; I was *supposed* to be there. It was awkward, but I was young enough for people to dismiss it, and old enough for me to understand that this was not typical behaviour.

As I got older, I grew bolder. In conversations about death with my grandmother, Nanny Alice, I challenged her, telling her I knew heaven was not a star.

"It's just a satellite," I said. "Nothing more."

She looked at me, her eyes seeking something in my own.

"Heaven is wherever you want it to be."

"Heaven is not a place," I pushed. "It's just where people go after. A place people like you can't see. But I can. I see it."

Her hands came together in her lap, squeezing. Her mouth opened and closed like a fish in water. She shifted her eyes, focusing on the family photos hanging on the living room wall.

"Well, then," she said before standing up and walking away from me. Death was not something she wanted to discuss. Grampy had hanged himself, and her response indicated that it was too painful for her to hear anything more about him.

Not long after that conversation, my Nanny Alice, my mother, and I were sitting at the kitchen table, talking about the kinds of things that filled time. Meaningless topics, what we would now call shooting the shit. The smoky and sweet smell of chicory coffee wafted from their mugs. For once, Nanny and Mom were not fighting, united in their grief after my Grampy died. I didn't know that others couldn't sense or feel him, so it felt like the most natural thing to share what he was saying to me.

"Grampy says..." I started, then filled them in on what Grampy was telling me. I gave them details about things that happened long before I was even born. The next thing I knew, I was being shuffled off to bed.

I lay under my covers, trying to figure out what had just happened. The curtains in front of my window were worn, making them almost transparent. Through the delicate fabric I could see the Big Dipper. Bright stars, all of them, but not heaven.

No one ever talked to me about Grampy again. And for once, I didn't ask questions. I knew what I saw and heard and that what I needed to say made people uncomfortable, like a kid picking their nose and eating it.

I know now that I can say whatever I want and share what I know and feel from Spirit, but not everyone will be ready for it.

By 2014, a few years into my career as a medium, I realized I needed a place to send all my emotions and empathy. My work with families who have tragedy— whether it's an unexpected death, suicide, overdose, or murder—affects me. Having a spot to put my feelings, I believed, would allow me and the ones I sat with room for healing and movement in their life.

One night, I sat under a clear sky, looking at the stars. When my eyes landed on the Big Dipper, my need for my own brightest star became obvious. I chose a star just under the constellation. That was the place I was going to send all the stuff I needed to release. My own Spirit recycling depot. My gift to myself.

After 13 years of channelling those who have crossed, I know I would never have been able to continue without my star. It's not heaven, but it helps.

Let the Light In

Ring the bells that still can ring
Forget your perfect offering
There is a crack, a crack in everything
That's how the light gets in.
— Leonard Cohen

We've been brought up to believe that death is sad. We're supposed to walk around with a cloud hanging over our heads, plodding along morosely through our grief. It's a burden we are supposed to carry until someone else tells us it's okay to move on.

I call bullshit.

There are cultures around the world where death isn't viewed as the end of life, but the pathway to the next one. Death is met with reverence, celebration, and enlightenment. In some parts of the world, strangers take part in a death walk for people they have never met because it's a deed that will be rewarded in the next life.

Because death is so serious for most North Americans (at least the ones I've encountered), I made it my mission to change that as much as I can. That's why I bring my sense of humour and foul language to my shows and readings. In my work, it became very important to never lose the fun side of my personality when walking someone through their pain. I didn't want the heaviness of grief and a difficult situation to overshadow a learning experience.

I never used to swear in my earlier shows. I dressed in dress pants and a nice shirt, trying to make a good impression, but like those cute shoes you bought online, those clothes never quite fit. It became clear that in order for me to do what I do well, I had to do what I do as my full authentic self. How could I expect people to open up to Spirit if I was a closed book myself? I am more comfortable showing up in ripped jeans and a ball cap.

So, yeah, I swear, but I'm delivering the information with personality and I'm trying to reflect the personality of the Spirit that is presenting to me. Yeah, I'm looking at you, Spirit of random middle-aged man, who showed me he can guzzle a whole beer in a single pull.

At every reading in my office or during a show, you are getting Jennie unfiltered and unmedicated.

We should be celebrating Spirit connecting with the people who are still here. They push through because they need the person to whom they are connected to know something. Sometimes what they show me makes me swear more. I won't apologize or tone it down to protect sensitive ears. There are so many people lost in this life and my job is to let Spirit show up for them. It's far better to smile or giggle. To drop f-bombs. I'm not laughing at your grief, I'm trying to help you find a way to let the light in so you can heal.

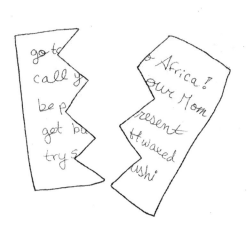

Abolish the List

If money and time were infinite, what would you do with that gift?

Almost everyone has the same answers when I ask this question.

1. Travel and
2. spend more time with loved ones.

We are all just borrowing time on this planet. So why waste it? We need to stop making a bucket list and start building an experience list. A bucket list is typically filled with desirable ideas and actions we feel are not achievable. An experience list should be populated with things you can accomplish in the short term. You have the intention, but haven't yet made the time.

These are not things like cleaning the toilet, walking the dog, or taking your books back to the library.

Experiences can change someone's day. Take your mom shopping and buy her a fancy bra. Pull your kid out of school and go out for lunch. Deliver a fancy coffee to your bestie in the middle of their work day.

These are the things people will remember and you'll be surprised at how much joy they can bring you too. Time is a valuable resource, spend it wisely.

TeeVee

Seeking Answers

We want to emulate the Oprahs and Brenés of this world. We watch them. We look to them for guidance. They are our lighthouses.

They teach us how to be better and do better at this living business. We have an arsenal of celebrities to walk us through all our moods. The ones that make us laugh. The ones that make us think. The ones we crush on. They remove us from our everyday lives and take us somewhere different. And that's fine as long as we never lose sight of the fact that these people are not our friends. Because we can only watch them from afar, they can never truly have a deep impact on our lives. Celebrities don't care what we post on Instagram.

Imagine if Spirit had access to your social media feeds. Actually, scratch that. Spirit *does* have the ability to show up wherever and whenever without a PR person, because Spirit is fluid energy. But until that happens for you, take some time to consider who the Oprahs and Brenés are in your own life. Who are the people who influence you to change for the better and raise you up?

The ones who help you dig into your inner Spirit and take a good hard look at who you are—those are your guides. Sometimes, our feelings manifest as admiration, while at other times, it comes out as discomfort.

Take stock of your people and really think about why you love them, listen to them, or let them get under your skin.

People come to me seeking answers from Spirit. They want assurances they are on the right path. They need advice on what choices to make. They may not like what they hear. It's not Spirit's job to tell you how to live your life. You'll have to work that out on your own. Connect with the living, breathing people around you, who love you and want to help.

Whatever you need to do, whatever books you need to read, do those things. Give yourself permission to hit rough patches. Never compare yourself to an Oprah or Brené because their journeys are different from yours. Stop focusing on the people who can't give you what you want. Focus instead on the people who give you what you need. Your life will be enriched, you'll be happier, and you'll form deeper connections—with Spirit, with the friends and family around you, and with yourself.

Show Up or Fuck Off

There's always a moment or two during a show when I connect with Spirit, but their loved one in the audience does not step up to accept the reading. I'll stand on the stage, or walk among the audience, repeating what Spirit is telling me, over and over, like the teacher in that famous movie calling "Bueller? Bueller?" to no response.

Listen, I'm there whether they answer the call or not. I can't control who comes through, but the strong ones always move to the front of the pack. The persistent fuckers won't stop nattering in my ear because they need to pass on a message. I always wonder why people buy tickets to a show with a medium and then try to shrivel into their seats when Spirit calls out for them. Did you not know what could happen?

A Spirit connection can be an absolute kick in the ass, but it can also offer you a subtle moment of clarity. It can offer you a chance to reset, to take a moment to understand where you've been and see the potential in where you can go. All you have to do is show up. From there, you can aim to do better. Take chances. Own your fuck-ups. Apologize. Accept and express gratitude.

I often have to remind people in a reading that if they had one year to live—to explore their greatness—

almost everyone would do it. You'd be crossing shit off your later list like there's no tomorrow, because in 365 days time's up.

The Devil Next Door

I once had a neighbour who took the time to open her door whenever she saw me leaving to greet me with her Jehovah's Witness special sauce. "You are the devil!" she would shout. At first, it was hurtful, but now, after being a medium for more than a decade, I know it was just her fear and her religion talking.

People land on one of two sides: they are either wholly fascinated with me or they walk away. People don't understand what I do. You'd think that with my ability to talk to Spirit, I'd never be alone, but life as a medium can be very lonely. I've had people shut down in the middle of a conversation as soon as they hear I'm a medium. Some folks freak out or ignore me completely. A lot of curious individuals will ask questions. It makes me sad when people run away from me or won't let me cross the threshold into their homes like I'm a blood-sucking vampire. Fear can, and will always, cripple you.

I have spent a lot of time trying to figure out who I am. It turns out I'm a human being who has challenges and limitations. I have to work on my shit too. I've finally reached the stage in life where I'm okay being the person who doesn't care what others think. It's not my job—and neither is it yours—to make people comfortable in their own insecurities. What matters to me is the knowledge that only I can wear my shoes, that my presence on this planet is valuable, as is yours.

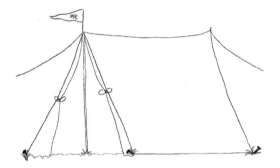

The Beginning of Me

After moving through foster care, struggling in my first year of university, and coping with being raped, I found a job that took me as far away as I could get from all that I knew. At 19 years old, I left Halifax with $17, a backpack, and a job at a campground thousands of kilometres away in Tofino. I was scared. I was getting on a plane, going to where I knew nobody and nobody knew me. Beyond landing in Nanaimo, I had no idea where I was going to end up or how I was going to get to where I was heading. I had to rely on myself. I had to push my doubts aside and just let things happen.

That was the beginning of me. That was the start of my life. My story started there.

My story is not that my mother was an alcoholic and abuser. That's her story. Your story isn't about the things other people did to you. How you were raised doesn't have to determine your narrative. How you were treated is an excuse to hold back on really living. How you emerge from your experience is your story.

My emergence came when I stepped off that plane, ready for adventure, shitting my pants over taking a risk and my fear of the unknown. I had to let go of everything familiar. Whatever happened from this day forward would be all on me. I was free. There would be no witness to my fuck-ups. There were no other people to mark the milestones or remind me of the failures in my life. I'd have to buy my own cake to celebrate my wins.

When you find yourself at the beginning of you, you'll be hyper-aware of all the ways you've held back. It's not easy to silence the voices and find who you really are. It's easier to remember the things that weren't and we fight like hell to avoid repeating those behaviours. What happens is we spend more time being not like the people who hurt us instead of exploring ourselves.

In doing the work I do, people are always trying to reach into the past for answers. They want Spirit to give them answers to their outstanding questions. *Should I take that job? Is this the right person for me to marry? Did I tell you I love you enough? Why did you do the things you did?*

Listen, there are a lot of unknowns in this world and we tend to look to the past to validate our choices. When you stop reaching to the past for answers, you will become more aware of what you need to do to change. Changing your inner dialogue—and boy, are we in an epidemic of negative dialogue—is the key to changing your story.

Take the time to understand who you are and examine what kind of life you're living. If you can break the chains of how you were raised, you will begin the shift to yourself. You will begin writing your own story.

Jennie's Gems

ADJUST, EXPERIENCE, ADAPT,
ADJUST AGAIN.

Getting Grounded

Go ahead. Take your shoes off. It's okay if your feet smell. There is not one person on the planet who hasn't had stinky feet at some point in their lives.

Look down. Your feet have carried you to new places. They can just as easily move you away from where you no longer want to be.

Our feet carry the burden of movement, an amazing feat given our feet only have 26 bones each. We squeeze them into shoes that are too small. We force them into itchy socks. We get the toes painted, heels scraped of dead skin.

It's time to let them get dirty. Feel the grass under your feet. Let them sink into the squish of mud. There are more than 14,000 nerve endings in your feet. Let them live a little.

All my life, I've been hovering, not knowing where to put my feet. I've roamed. I've tried different careers. When you are restless, without direction, feeling lost or deep in heartache, it's essential to ground yourself, starting the healing from the bottom.

There are 33 joints and more than 29 muscles in each foot doing the heavy lifting. They'll support you, just like they always have. Allowing ourselves to connect to the Earth from the ground up is powerful. It doesn't require any special skills or rituals. Just take your damn shoes off.

Rocking the Boat

If you were a kid in the 1970s and 1980s, Saturday night television was the best. My entire generation grew up with big dreams, big jewelry, and big love, presented to us weekly via *Fantasy Island*, *Dynasty*, and *The Love Boat*. I wanted to be Julie McCoy, the cruise director who orchestrated all the love connections. As a kid, I thought it was awesome, but now I realize she was directing people to hook up. As a pre-teen through to my teenage years, I wanted to be the fun, popular, Nova Scotian version of Julie.

Why wouldn't I get on a big-ass boat and be Julie McCoy for a while? Because I was petrified of the ocean. The thought of being far from shore at the mercy of Mother Nature and her big swells was terrifying. But my dream of being Julie on *The Love Boat* was bigger than my fear.

I worked hard to get that job. When I applied, I was working the overnight shift on the switchboard at a popular hotel in Banff. I was restless and seeking a way out. When you work in the tourism industry, you hear about job openings all the time, and when I had the chance to apply for a position on a cruise ship, I knew this was my chance to fulfil a dream I'd had since I was a little girl.

This girl from butt-fuck nowhere was given the chance to get out, something I never thought was possible. So with visions of walking around in a jacket and skirt, wearing comfy loafers and holding a clipboard, I flew to Boca Raton, Florida, to interview for a job on a cruise ship.

A few weeks later, I was offered the job! I was equally thrilled and terrified. I was going to work in guest relations, which was close enough to Julie's job as cruise director.

Julie was outgoing and friendly. She made people feel really great and I was going to do the same. She got to hang out around the pool, chatting with guests. She dressed up for dinners in fancy gowns. She always had a smile on her face. I practised my smile, preparing to deal in happiness and dream-making, all while getting to travel and see the world. This was a bucket list experience for me, something I could now move to the "I'm doing it" column.

By the end of my first shift, I realized *The Love Boat* was 100 percent fantasy. This was a much harder job than was portrayed in an hour-long episode. We worked 12-hour shifts, without any days off. My uniform was all I got to wear, every single day. Not a single gown! Working on a cruise ship is a nonstop grind. There was no laugh track and there were no romances for me to orchestrate. I don't regret a single day, though. I worked with a great crew. I met people from all over the world. And the ocean was not so scary after all.

I never thought I was good enough to be Julie, but I

was given the opportunity to try. Despite all my self-doubt, being afraid of the ocean, and my lack of experience, I put my whole heart into my work.

While I may not have had dinner with Captain Stubing or a fleeting romance with Gopher, I learned a lot about myself:

I discovered the fear of doing something is actually bigger than what you experience.

The thought of a wasp sting is worse than the actual sting.

I realized that when I put my full energy into achieving something, I can make it happen.

Call it manifestation, drive, intention, or whatever name you need to put to it. When you aim to be all in, great things will happen.

The Big Brick

I magine you've been in a horrible collision. Your car is a tangled mess, completely unrecognizable. The fire crew needed to use the Jaws of Life to extract you from the vehicle. The paramedics are ready, defibrillator paddles charged in case your heart stops. Once the door has been sheared off the frame, you step out of the car without a scratch. Time freezes. No one can understand how this happened. Everyone in emergency services has seen too many accident scenes like this one, where the medical coroner is the only one with a job to do. You should be dead, mangled, transferred into a black body bag.

As the days pass, the shock wears off, and the pain of the impact creeps into every part of your body. But your brain is alert, fully aware of what a lucky bastard you are.

What do you do now?

Close your eyes and imagine this scenario. Use all five senses to bring you into the moment. Then write down the two big actions that immediately come to mind after you emerge from this traumatic event. Not the practical actions like calling insurance and arranging for a rental car. What are the first two things you will do to make a positive change in your life? Once you've committed them to paper, place it somewhere where you will see those actions on a daily basis.

Take a photo and make it the wallpaper on your phone. If you see it, you can live it.

Did you choose to thank God for sparing you because you have to go to work and support your family? That is not a big enough gesture. Saying a silent prayer is not any different than avoiding running over a squirrel. Once your heart slows and the squirrel is safely across the road, you can carry on, as you were.

Someone who walks away from a disastrous accident has to allow themselves the brain space to think about why they got to walk away when others were not that lucky.

You don't need to bargain or beg for direction. You've been granted the gift of life. You now have a chance to do better. You have dreams and aspirations that matter. Your work here in this world is not done.

People often have to go through a huge experience, usually traumatic, in order to *wake the fuck up*.

The trauma is not necessary. You have the capacity to make a change at any time in your life. You don't need to wait for a big brick to hit you. Your personal transformation can happen at any time. On a Monday. Or after lunch. Or hiking in the woods.

Change is scary, but you can't be brave if you are not scared.

Pickles and a Rant

I f you don't like pickles, I'm sorry, but we can't be friends.

I'm kidding of course. I love pickles. Crunchy. Salty. Wet. Sorry if that grosses you out. It could have been worse. I could have said ... moist.

But jokes aside, I started eating pickles and ranting in a video on Facebook, because at any given time my brain fills with things I wonder about and I wanted a space to talk about life, death, and whether Smurfs have teeth.

I use Facebook as a place to answer the most common questions I get. Here is the short summary of the hot topics I cover. Grab a pickle and join me.

People always—*always*—want to know what it's like to be a medium. Do I hear voices all the time? (Only when my kid wants money.) Can I see into the future? (Check my bank balance for your answer.) Heaven forbid my eyes travel over someone's shoulder when I am talking to them, because then they want to know what I'm looking at.

Here's the thing: Whenever I walk into a new situation—say, a social event—and someone asks me what I do for a living, I have to pause. Do I pretend to be an insurance agent, or do I candidly tell a complete stranger what I do? I'm not embarrassed about my work, but I never know what the reaction will be.

Believe it or not, as many people find what I do intriguing as those who get creeped out. Sometimes, people shut down immediately, and among that group are people who suddenly don't know how to make their mouths work anymore, and people who have no issue wagging their tongues and telling me exactly where I am going and who I am working for. ("Hell" and "the devil," in case I lost you.)

Let me explain what being a medium is *not*. I am not always on. I am not perpetually listening for Spirit. I know Spirit is all around me all the time, but mediums can turn it off at will. Like a light switch or a water tap. I don't operate like a Ouija board or a Magic 8 Ball. I cannot see into your future. I don't know what you are thinking. I will never walk up to someone and force my knowledge on you. Spirit may be nudging me, but if you don't ask, I won't tell. That would be like a hairdresser standing in line behind you at the grocery store and telling you what you should be doing with your hair. Even I would think, "That's a crazy person" and take a few steps away.

"What do you see around me?" is a question I am asked a lot, as if I walk around channelling 24/7. I see trees and flowers. I see a 60-year-old woman rocking skinny jeans. I see dog shit on the sidewalk. I'm not any different from anyone else. I experience life as you do. I feel excited about new things. My heart gets broken. I get angry over injustice.

People have often told me they themselves were

connected to Spirit but shut it down because it was too scary or overwhelming. You can't shut down Spirit or energy. You can't stop it. What they're actually saying is, "I'm shutting down any and all things I can't control."

They picked control over energy. Toss that around in your head for a bit. They are actually limiting themselves from allowing life to happen without expectation.

I ask these people, "Tell me, how do you shut it off?" They never tell me how, they simply tell me that they don't want it turned on. I find myself wondering what they gain by ignoring Spirit and what emotions they are avoiding.

Sure, I can sense your energy and that of Spirit, but I don't much care when I'm not working. It takes effort to find balance in life, regardless of what you do for a living. Some of us can turn the computer off at the end of the day, dimming the office lights as we close the door. Others cannot leave the work behind when they walk out the door. I am always alert, looking for ways to make the world better, not just for my clients, but for my daughter as well. For all those I love and have loved. My connection to Spirit isn't something to drown out or ignore. It's a deeply ingrained part of me. It's who I have always been. Without being a medium, I am still Jennie.

Bedtime Thoughts with Jennie

I'm not embarrassed to say that for the longest time, I could not understand what racing cars had to do with dead animals. I misheard the word "taxidermy" as "taxiderby" and struggled to find the connection between taxis racing around a track and stuffed carcasses on display. I also wonder who thought stuffing roadkill would make nice decorative accessories for the home. I'm so glad that someone had the forethought to draw the line when it comes to stuffing loved ones to keep in your home.

At night, my brain seems to revert to the curiosity of a child. Children are the best at asking random questions at the most inopportune times. You might be sitting down for a church service when an eight-year-old blurts out, "Mommy, what is a whore?" Or maybe while you're enrolling your child in kindergarten, they might say, "Mommy, do you think this teacher has a beard on her bottom like you do?" Children have zero filter, and sometimes neither do I.

My brain fires off in many different directions as I'm winding down for the day, settling into the sheets for sleep. My mind circles with questions, many of which I wouldn't want to blurt out loud in public as conversation starters.

Here are some of my more nonsensical concerns:

Do Smurfs have teeth?

Where do bees go in winter?

Why are they called *ham*burgers when they are made with beef?

When did car manufacturers sneak in the fuel tank arrow telling us which side the gas tank is on?

Why is the English language so confusing with so many words that sound exactly the same, but have very different meanings? When someone says, "Let's touch base," I can't be sure it's not an invitation to play baseball. Or play the guitar. Don't even get me started on "bologna."

English is so complicated. If we can't even understand the language, how can we understand ourselves?

Jennie's Gems

*NOT DOING ANYTHING IS EVERYTHING
YOU IMAGINED IT WOULD BE.*

Choose a Lane

There is the saying that people don't change, but I think that is utter bullshit. Another popular saying that is garbage is that everything you needed to know you learned in kindergarten. If I stopped learning new things in kindergarten, then I would never have figured out I was a lesbian and I would have grown up to become a fire truck. It would have been a shame to have missed out on some valuable life lessons and getting to know myself if I let five-year-old me shut down the learning.

Life is a series of connections, a cosmic connect-the-dots. The people we meet, the places we go, the lessons we learn (or ignore) are all necessary pieces of our life experience. Every connection serves a purpose. Connections form who we are, giving us the tools we need to persevere, because we are not the same person in every situation.

How you cope when someone rear ends you at a traffic light is very different from how you'd respond to a surprise party. A broken heart provokes different actions than a broken bone. When we are fully steeped in valuable connections, paying attention to our instincts and the lessons we've learned, we are better prepared to manage even the most emotional events.

We can't be afraid to be who we truly are because someone else expects us to act in a certain way. We spend a majority of our lives pleasing other people until we don't want to do that anymore. Many people have ended up sitting on the couch in the safe space of my office, wanting to talk about how they hate pleasing people.

We try to be nice to a boss who acts without fairness or integrity because they hold our employment in their hands. We let bad friends hang around, compromising our own values. We stay with a spouse long after love has died. When a family member dies, people collect together out of a sense of obligation, not necessarily because they want to appreciate the time the person had on Earth. It's a fragile connection to the physical being that is severed the minute the funeral ends.

Not all connections are so weak. The ones we choose are the ones that can make us better people. Your chosen family is made up of the few handpicked people to whom you gravitate. You find value in each other and there is a balance between giving and taking. These people wholeheartedly have your back and you would give them the shirt off of yours. You can call out each other's bullshit and force each other out of a safe —but boring—comfort zone. They make you laugh till you cry or pee your pants.

Building strong connections and finding your people is like weeding a garden. No one likes the shit that is not supposed to be there, so we get rid of it. If a blood-sucking, energy-draining person like that exists in your life, deadhead them. This makes room for good things to grow and flourish.

We all experience loss in our life, whether it be death, a dead-end relationship, or an empty friendship. But it's okay. Feeling grief and heartache means you are growing. It's not failure, it's planting seeds for beautiful things. We outgrow people, just like we outgrow shoes, clothing, and even our smartphones. At some point, these things don't work the way we need them to. Don't be tempted to take the familiar road when it no longer serves you. Own your growth. Dump the bad connections. Choose the lane that inspires you to live.

Pinkie Finger Swear

The simple secret of the law of attraction is this: you attract what you *are*, not what you want.

Keep your thoughts positive, because your thoughts become your words.
Keep your words positive, because your words become your behaviours.
Keep your behaviours positive, because your behaviours become your habits.
Keep your habits positive, because your habits become your values.
Keep your values positive, because your values become your destiny.

— Gandhi

You are the source of your own happiness. Make a pinkie finger swear with yourself to be your authentic self, to live *as you* are, not who others want you to be.

Ancestry is Not Family

I t's a really cool thing to be able to pop onto the computer and find your ancestors. As a child looking to escape my reality, I always suspected I was related to royalty. Deep down inside my own heart, there was strength and confidence, completely appropriate for someone descendant from kings and queens. I imagined I'd be able to trace my lineage back hundreds of years, to the Middle Ages of England, where my kith and kin spent their days behind castle walls, drinking wine and lounging as much as their corsets would allow.

But when I actually did the research I learned that I, like most Nova Scotians, am descended from the French and the English. That means my ancestors went heavy on alcohol and debauchery, had big mouths, and did lots of screaming. Seems right. Fuck.

Ancestry, though, is not family. These are very different things. Ancestry is tied to blood lines, while family is tied to stories. There can be a lot of folklore in families. In my own family, the stories were buried, ignored, and hidden. Over time and generations, stories will change and details will be lost. Family lore is the ultimate broken Telephone.

Imagine finding out the precious 100-year-old heir-loom you've always loved was actually a piece of shit mass-manufactured in a factory. You'd be heartbroken because you've been lied to your entire life. Unless your ancestors were from China.

Your ancestors are far removed from who you are today, by centuries or millennia. Your family is made of tangible people: the ones you touch, hug, and trust. And that gives them incredible power to hurt you. Your parents will mould you with their views of the world. They will infuse you with their own ideas. From your family members, you will learn how to behave, react, respond, and absorb. I'll go out on a limb here and say everyone has some emotional stunting they inherited from family members. They can hurt us by transferring their own fears onto us, squashing our dreams and filling our heads with their own insecurities.

Even the kindest of families have a black sheep. It can manifest as the theatrical cousin who shuns the athletic nature of the rest of the family, or it can show up as simply the desire to do something different from what is expected. Being the black sheep is not always a bad thing, especially if you are trying to do what is right for *you*.

I see this in so many of the people who come to me for a reading. They are unsettled, not just because of the loss of a loved one, but because they let the voices of others into their brains.

Some of this might sound familiar:

"I should have been there at the end."

"I should have said I love you more often."

"I don't think I gave them the funeral/burial/last rites they wanted."

These words become part of the family story, a consciousness that has been woven so deep through generations, no one has dared to question them. It's not easy to be the one who speaks up or who moves in a different direction. Your grief and your guilt should be managed in a way that feels right for you. There will be pain. There will be heartbreak. But you have to give yourself permission to break free of the ancestral myth and the issues of other members of your family. It's okay that you weren't there to witness the last breath. It's fine that you didn't indebt yourself for a funeral. And it's 100 percent okay to not close out every conversation with "I love you" if you said it yesterday or if the sentiment is not genuine. Your risk-taking ancestors would have done whatever the fuck they wanted. Let the bloodlines be your guide.

Spirit and Suicide

Content Warning: This chapter deals with the loss of adult children, spousal abuse, and suicide.

There's something really special about the change of seasons from spring to summer. The breeze feels warmer, the sun stays out longer, and I swear you can sometimes *smell* things growing. Good things. Green things. Things that are so very much alive.

That was the kind of Saturday it was when I was getting ready for a 4 p.m. reading. The sun was still high enough in the sky that it wasn't yet peeking uncomfortably through the blinds in my office. I could leave them open, and neither me nor my client would be blinded. With the promise of summer lightening my step, I puttered around my office, tidying things up and making sure I was ready for my appointment.

As soon as I opened the door for my client, I felt immediately overwhelmed with sadness and an entire wave of nausea. That was my sign that this was going to be a pretty intense reading.

This woman had suffered unbearable loss. Her 21-year-old son had been killed instantly in a car accident. Two weeks after that accident, her husband dropped dead of a heart attack. And four weeks after that her daughter committed suicide. She had come to me looking for answers about the afterlife.

While she was sitting on my couch wondering aloud what hope is, her husband came through and whispered two words to me.

"She's next."

He was telling me that her intention, once she received confirmation of Spirit being real, was to go home and take her own life.

I looked at this broken woman who was looking down at her hands in her lap, surrounded by grief and despair and bluntly said, "So, you want to go and join them, huh?"

"Yes," she answered, barely loud enough for me to hear. "I have no reason to be here."

"Your husband is telling me you have plans to commit suicide when you go home. He's showing me that you have everything ready. That it's all planned out. And he also tells me that this is your last stop because there's a part of you that doesn't believe energy survives past life, that there's life after death. Your family has come through to give you validations that they are very much with you. They are showing up because it's not your time."

She fell silent. I've seen this before, where someone is suspended between wanting to believe and not wanting to let themselves believe. It's totally in line with someone who doesn't want to face the music, to actively take responsibility for the way life has turned out.

"You don't want to be here, but how is that going to fix anything?" I asked.

"I don't want to fix anything," she answered.

I felt the fire of frustration bubble up inside my chest. I wanted to yell at her, to tell her that ending her life at 7 p.m. was not the answer, that death around us was meant to move us toward more life.

She was still looking at her hands in her lap, now busy folding and twisting a tissue.

I spoke softly. "You're so focused on your grief that not once have you stopped to think about why *you* are still here. I'm not here to stop you. I'm here to encourage you to look at things differently."

Our conversation changed after that.

While she was still hell bent on suicide, she was ready to share her pain openly. She had never been on her own, ever, and didn't think she could do it. She didn't see her own worth, and was stuck listening to the words of her verbally abusive husband on autoplay inside her head. Her son was responsible for his own fatal accident. Her daughter lost her life from using drugs to dull the pain of loss.

All three of her loved ones came through to tell me her secrets. My client was living a lie, such a big lie that she didn't think she could move on, find her worth, her passion, or her power. All she could see was hopelessness and loneliness. The façade of her life had broken apart with each death and now here she sat, in my office, with nothing but suicide between her and facing the shit of her life.

At the end of the appointment, I told her, "If you're still here next week, give me a shout. Take care." It might sound harsh to push her out the door, but there is nothing I can do that will stop someone from taking their own life if they are determined. She left her session knowing she was fully responsible for what-ever outcome she chose. I can't change her mind, but I can guide her to a better understanding of death and help her figure out all the reasons she has to live.

Thoughts of suicide following the death of a loved one aren't only driven by loss and grief. It's you not taking ownership and accepting the time you'll never get back. But let me be perfectly clear about some-thing. This feeling of failure and despair is not guilt. Guilt is often associated with losing someone, but when you delve deeper into the feeling, you'll under-stand that you are overwhelmed.

Guilt is defined as the state of committing an offense or violating the law or a feeling of deserving blame for offences. You might not believe me because they're such bedfellows, but guilt and death do not go together. You have not done anything wrong or illegal. You have committed no offence. You are merely over-whelmed by the death you have experienced.

Regret and death—now that's a whole different story. You can have regret for the things not said or done, for not telling someone you love them, or for not taking steps to rectify the emotional scars you carry. There will always be something you don't have that you want. There will always be unexpected loss. Death cannot be controlled or put in a calendar and scheduled. Death should be your wake-up call to fix the unhealthy patterns in your life.

When someone you love dies, pay attention to how you deal with death, because that will show you the patterns you use to deal with life.

Do you want to curl up and hide?

Do you blame everyone else for your losses?

Are you lashing out, stuck, or keeping busy?

Death is an emotional hemorrhoid that will make things even worse when you shit your pants. It points you to where you need to be invested in your life. Death makes you 100 percent show up for your emotions. It shines a bright light on all the dirt you've been sweeping under the carpet.

Death, when viewed through the lens of living a good life, is just a period at the end of your sentence. What sentence you write to make your life matter is entirely up to you.

My client from that warm Saturday did call me a couple of weeks after we met. She began the work of fixing what wasn't working in her life, and it was a long list. She is still with us today, thriving and investing in living.

A Glass of Water

Content Warning: This chapter deals with rape, pedophilia, and child abuse.

In the mildew stink of the arena dressing room, three dresses hung awkwardly from their white plastic hangers. The institutional grey of the walls, the lockers, and the benches looked even more worn against the soft, flowing taffeta of these dresses. Not many young women came through here in pastel-coloured, puffy-shouldered dresses. I was going to wear each of those dresses that day: one for my speech, one for the formal gown, and one for the talent portion. They were all secondhand, but they all had one thing in common: they made me feel good, at least for a short period of time.

I won Miss Talent and Miss Friendship in those dresses. I was crowned Princess Kentville in the soft pink, big-shouldered taffeta. If we had the language of today back in 1989, I would have said, "Best. Day. Ever."

My start in life had not been easy. From my crib to my foster home, bad things happened to me. My mother couldn't nail down who my father was because she was probably drunk at the time. She partied. She slept around. She was physically violent. She went to prison. Unsure of herself as a woman and a mother, she pushed me through a revolving door into places where very bad men could plant themselves in my life. I was left alone with a known pedophile, abused by an "uncle" (not a family member), and fondled by a family friend while I floated in a tube on the dark waters of a lake. Later, as a young woman, I was roofied and raped. Everything about my youth pointed to me repeating the cycle of abuse and molestation.

Yet here I am today. A woman who is sure of who she is, despite what she could have been. I won't bore you with the heartbreak or the disappointments in my life. That's boring shit. We all have garbage we need to deal with.

As a child, I dealt with my pain by banging my head against the wall. Literally. I smacked my lid against chairs, walls, and cement. It was the only way I knew how to defuse my anger and frustration. I was hurting and alone. But I always knew this was not the only way for me. I intuitively knew this was just a leg on my journey and I was going to move past it. Eventually.

Stick with me and play along for a second. If I hold up a glass of water and ask you what you see, you'll tell me "water." If I do that two more times and you still only see a glass of water, you are a repeater. This is a lesson you can apply to any part of your life. If you have financial problems and keep spending on things you want but don't need, you'll always be in debt. You are never going to get out of the rut. You will keep fighting. You will keep banging your head against the wall. If you let fear keep you stuck, you will never move forward.

When you see the same thing three different ways, I can tell you that you are going to be okay. The glass of water can be a refreshment, a source of life, or a way to get the sauce you dripped off your boob shelf. When you take a good hard look at your spending patterns, you might be able to see that your need to buy things is filling an emotional hole or giving you the opportunity to be generous (sometimes to the wrong people) or showing you an opportunity to save money. You will eventually find clarity and a way out of the shit you're currently in. Change is not hard. You can get past whatever you've been through, or what you are going through, or what is locking you into misery.

It's never just a glass of water.

Jennie's Gems

SEND YOURSELF AN INVITATION TO MOVE FORWARD FROM GRIEF.

Palm Trees

Nanny Alice was my biggest fan. She stuck her neck out for me when I needed her and stuck her nose in even when I didn't want the attention. This was not always a bad thing.

When I found out I was pregnant at 31 years old, my anxiety kicked into high gear. I was alone, a lesbian, and lost about how I was going to explain how this happened. Following an ultrasound, I was told the fetus was showing signs of Down syndrome.

With my mother checked out of my life, I only had my grandmother, Nanny Alice, to talk to.

"I don't know if this is going to be okay," I said.

"Buffy, whatever shall be, shall be." Yeah, that's my nickname. Everyone in Nova Scotia calls me Buffy. Now all the world knows.

I knew I had no option but to take care of myself. This was probably the only time I was going to be pregnant. I was going to have to figure out how to manage being a single mom to a special needs baby. I was terrified, depressed, and drifting.

When another round of tests came back clear, indicating there was no Down's, the fear gripping my chest released. I was going to be okay. Nanny Alice's "what shall be" became Shelby.

My grandmother was a colourful and important presence in my life. As I floundered, trying to figure out my life, she was there in the background, waiting for me when I was ready. When my mother went to jail, she became the one person in my life I could count on being around.

Having never really travelled, Nanny Alice used to tell me palm trees didn't exist. So when I flew to Puerto Rico to start working on the cruise ship, I mailed her a photo of me standing in front of a real palm tree. It was important to me that she knew they truly existed and that I, too, now knew they were the real deal.

When life wore her down near the end, I spent 10 days with her, feeding and nursing her. I was on full-time potty and poop duty. We had great conversations about life, love, and palm trees.

"Keep doing what you're doing and settle for nothing," she instructed me.

"What do you mean, Nanny?"

"You have no excuses. Ruffle feathers. People will listen. Who cares about the ones that don't?"

In a shallow breath, she added, "You be you."

Those were her last words to me before she passed. I left her bedside to go back to living my life out west. Nanny Alice was my greatest loss.

My grandmother, Alice Lillian Ogilvie, died at 78 years old knowing she didn't have to worry about me. I didn't return to Nova Scotia for the celebration of her life. My celebration was me spending time with her, giving her medicine, taking care of her, and just talking about some good times. I knew her living, not dead. That's how I choose to remember her.

I don't grieve for her. I meet with her. We talk, we connect, and I know the trueness of her.

"You be you" plays in my head constantly. That one sentence allowed me to know there was one person on my side. Nanny Alice got me.

If you do shit that makes people uncomfortable (without being an asshole), do not stop because of them.

You be you.

If you find yourself doing things to please others at the cost of your own happiness, please stop.

You be you.

Say what you mean and mean what you say.

You be you.

Take ownership of making your mark in this world because no one else will.

Add to your story. Be bold. Be unconventional. Be you.

Let Your Mind Wonder and Wander

I sit on the beach, watching the waves come in and then recede. The motion is hypnotic, the sound reaching deep into my soul. With every wave, the landscape changes. The sand is pulled away to reveal rocks and shells I didn't see a moment ago. The algae rides the crest of the waves, getting left behind to paint nature's patterns on the shore, much like clouds decorate the sky. Over there, to the left of my baby toe, the seaweed looks like a feather boa. Right in front of me, the bright sun plays tricks with the algae, making it look dark green one moment and then neon blue the next.

The beach is forever shifting and changing, just like we all are. With every rush of water or the gentle whooshing of the breeze through the trees, I can feel the shift. If I close my eyes, I can sort the stress from the joy. It's just me and my mind, working through my shit. That's why so many people flock to the ocean. We tell ourselves we need to get out of the cold and find some warmth so winter doesn't feel so long. But we are liars.

What we really need is time to step out of our lives. We need to spend time within ourselves.

You don't need a beach to do this kind of internal work. You can do this anywhere. I can look up at the night sky off a country road and count the stars at the same time as I count my blessings. I can throw my arms up to a cloudy sky and take a moment to feel the awareness of what I am and what I'm doing. I understand that life is bigger than my physical eyes and physical body. Life has no parameters, just an infinity of awareness. Awareness is not merely what we know by happenstance. Awareness is about understanding what is available to know.

I dance under the big sky and say, "Hey world! Do you see me? I am doing this!"

Let me put this simply: let your mind wonder and wander. Think about the big things, but remove the structure of linear thought. Allow your thoughts to be fragmented and give your mind room to figure out what the heck you are trying to do. From the chaos comes clarity.

There is no right or wrong way to do this. Your feet are not planted, they are available for an adventure. All you need to do is be open to the experience. Like meditation, change will take practice. Start wanting more for yourself. Take the first step. Let the random, broken thoughts come. Take a deep breath. Let your mind wander.

Yellow Rain Boots

I didn't own a pair of rain boots until I was an adult. People don't actually believe me when I tell them that, since I grew up in Nova Scotia.

"How do you live on the East Coast and not have rain boots?" they'll ask.

It's simple really. When I was growing up in Nova Scotia, there was no money for rubber boots, even in a place where it rains, on average, 161 days per year. We shopped in secondhand stores and I wore hand-me-downs all the time. We didn't go for haircuts; Nanny Alice took shears to our manes.

So when I found myself at age 19, working in a campground in Tofino—also known as the "wet coast"—with money in my pocket, owning a pair of rainboots was suddenly a viable reality. I didn't just buy any old rain boots, I bought yellow ones. And not just run-of-the-mill discount store yellow boots.

I bought the good shit: Helly Hansen.

I needed these Hellys to keep my feet dry. I treated myself to something deluxe for the first time. I was used to scraping money together, and living from paycheque to paycheque, but on this, I was not willing to compromise.

When I took my first walk in those boots, there was pep in my step. These boots made me happy, and I soon realized it was an internal happiness. I had overcome adversity, survived abuse, and made something of my life. I had moved across the country, left my old life and self behind. I had every reason to smile.

With every step I took in those boots, I was getting stronger, but I was still finding out who I was and where I fit in. There was more work to do. But at least my feet would be dry.

Foster Home

I woke up in a field the morning of the day my life started to get better.

The previous night, I had run to get away from my mother. She had threatened to kill herself and I shrugged and told her to do what she had to do. As I slammed the door behind me, I could hear her screaming that I was the reason she drank and I was the reason she beat me. I had nothing left to give. There was nothing left for me there. I wandered through town, trying to figure out what I was going to do. There was no safe place for me, and so I dropped onto the field, emotionally and physically exhausted.

The field where I woke up was in an undeveloped part of Kentville, not far from my house. On my nighttime flight from my mother's house, I had managed to find a spot in the field that was more lawn than dirt and chose it as my bed. I shuddered from the chill when I stood up, the ground and my clothes both damp from the spring dew. My body left a gentle dent in the new grass. My hair was flattened on one side. I prayed my clothes would be dry by the time school started. Maybe no one would know I had slept outdoors.

My friend Lisa knew, though, as soon as she saw me. Lisa told her dad, an industrial arts teacher at the school, and before lunch I was in the principal's office listening to these adults make a plan. Because it was not safe for me to stay with my mother, I was to stay at Lisa's house until a foster home could be arranged.

A week later, my transition into a foster home was tacked on to the end of my school day like an extracurricular activity. I was instructed to return to my mother's house, but only to get my things. My mother was home, sitting in her spot on the couch. She didn't say anything, nor did she acknowledge what was happening. When my back was turned, I felt the heat of her angry glare, knowing that she was blaming me for what was happening. I knew she would spin the story she told others, complaining that she was embarrassed by the drama I created.

As we turned left just beyond the town limits of Wolfville, Nova Scotia, I couldn't yet see the house that would be my new home. The driveway was long and curved. I sat in the back seat without emotion. I wasn't scared or excited. I wasn't eager or feeling lost. I was numb.

Andrea and Tony, my new foster parents, were clearly not expecting a new child that night. The porch light was on at the two-storey house they had built themselves and, from the car, I could hear music and laughter, sounds I never heard enough of. When my guardian rang the doorbell, I could see a silhouette through the glass in the front door. The woman who opened the door smiled as her eyes passed over me, but I saw a look of confusion flash over her face. She recovered quickly. I would soon learn that Andrea was quintessentially German: precise, stern, and able to mask emotions with ease.

Andrea and Tony's house was filled with guests that night. I was dropped off the same night their friends threw them a surprise 25th wedding anniversary celebration. To add to the surprise, while they had signed up to be foster parents to a child between the ages of eight and nine, they now had a moody, wild, and difficult-to-live-with 15-year-old on their doorstep.

I was welcomed into the home immediately. Andrea guided me into the living room and introduced me as their new foster daughter. I melted into the party, listening to the bits of conversation, trying to absorb the surroundings. There were books and CDs everywhere. I looked at some of the music albums with names I couldn't pronounce: Tchaikovsky, Rachmaninoff, Beethoven. On the kitchen counter stood corked and uncorked bottles of wine and real crystal wine glasses. Some of the guests spoke with accents and many of them, I discovered later, were fellow professors at Acadia University. They were well put together: clean slacks or long skirts, soft shirts with buttons or flowing sleeves, draped scarves or neat ties. I have arrived, I thought to myself, and I was going to be smart after living here. These were the kind of people I hoped one day to emulate.

The things in this house were so foreign to me. Exotic foods like couscous. Spices that didn't come from the dollar store. Dark rye bread. Fresh fruits and vegetables in the fridge. The plates we ate off matched and were china, not the assorted Corelle unbreakable dishes I was familiar with. We put our drinks on coasters and had magazines like *The Economist* and *Maclean's* to read. Plants adorned all the vacant spaces in the house, soaking up the sunshine that always seemed to find its way into my new home. People from all over the world came over for dinner. I knew these were smart people from the way they talked and the words they used. I remember feeling like I was around sophisticated people, people who didn't wear Avon perfume.

"One day," I said to myself, "I'm going to make sure my life is so interesting that people are going to want to sit down and talk to me."

For the first time in my life, I had a bedroom to call my own, a room I didn't have to share with anybody. I no longer had to sleep on a couch. My room had a slanted cathedral ceiling, bookshelves, and lamps from Ikea. I had someone to lovingly tuck me in at night.

There was so much structure in that house. They wanted to talk about things and sit down together for supper. There was a specified bedtime. Andrea and Tony had a reasonable expectation that I would be respectful and do my chores. My job was to mow the lawn, a large area that extended from the back of the house to the front. There was a lot of lawn.

I was only with Andrea and Tony for a few months before I bailed and went back to my mother. I never really gave the foster home a fair chance. They had no idea who I was. You can't put an abnormal kid into a normal environment and expect her to thrive. I didn't really know how to communicate and would shut down, not talking for days. I wasn't used to being hugged or being acknowledged for who I was. It's hard to fit in when you've spent most of your youth surrounded by the broken bits and pieces of other people.

All my life I've been hovering, not sure where to put my feet. I was dropped off wherever it was convenient for my mom. I had moved 32 times before I started Grade 12. My life was always in motion. I was running from my mother, from people who hurt me. I often spent weekends with teachers who took me in so I could have a safe place to study and a glimpse of a life other than the violent one I knew. I am one of the lucky ones who always had someone there for me. I was surrounded by people who saw the bright light in me and wanted to give me the opportunity to shine.

It was all those people who helped me get past my emotions. My anger is done now. I look back at the lessons I learned, not just from those who tried to protect me, but also from those who raised their hands to harm me. What they taught me was that I had the power to stand up for myself, to aspire to great things and to make better choices. It was this freedom, and my constant need for motion that sent me running to start a different part of life.

The Power of No

"No." It's a complete sentence that holds a lot of power. As toddlers, it's one of the first words we learn and we typically yell it out. For the next three to five years, it's a word children use to express desire, defiance, and independence. As parents, we move from encouraging this personality development to trying to stifle it with our own set of rules. Then, when we send our kids off to school, we teach them to scream "NO!" when a stranger tries to touch them, but not to say no when the teacher tells them to practise their letters.

It's little wonder that when we grow up we have no idea how to properly use the word. The power of "no" fades when we give away little pieces of ourselves, become people pleasers and put the needs and wants of others before our own. The protectionist ability gets lost in a sea of doubt.

For my whole childhood and adolescence, people told me how to act, but I always coloured outside the lines. It was frustrating for me to try to fit into a mould that wasn't mine and it was frustrating to those who were constantly arguing and fighting with me. So I bent like a small tree in a strong wind. For years, I didn't know I had it in me to say "NO!" and "IT'S NOT OKAY."

As I got older, I finally recognized I needed to stop

caring how my own choices made other people feel. Saying "no" is the best state of being. It allows you to build strength from the inside. Saying "no" with the knowledge that you are protecting and not compromising yourself is scary as fuck, especially if you've been saying "yes" forever. The power of "no" is beautiful because it saves space for you and makes room for other experiences.

Saying "no" takes practice, like meditation. You'll suck at it at first. Every fibre in your being will pull you toward saying "yes," because that's as familiar as pulling on a stretched-out pair of holey underwear.

Roll "no" around your mouth and your brain. See how it fits. Once you and "no" are comfortable, guard it as if your life depends on it.

Jennie's Gems

JUST BECAUSE THE ROAD AHEAD IS UNCLEAR
DOESN'T MEAN IT'S THE WRONG ROAD.

Find the Lighthouses

I spent a week in the summer after Grade 9 at a Baptist camp. Shocking, I know. I didn't feel like I was being punished or forced into a religion, though. One of my guardians at the time was a leader of a church youth group. Summer camp was an extension of the sense of belonging I got from the group. It was time outdoors, away from the everyday exhaustion of my life. There should really be a summer camp for adults, where we can make arts and crafts, play dodgeball, sleep on uncomfortable beds, and take the risk of drinking coffee at eight o'clock at night.

When summer camp was over, I went back to live with my mom. The heat of summer was still hanging in the air, but the humidity had started to level off. Every so often, a light breeze would push the air around and I could smell the earthy start of fall. While the leaves would change, nothing would be different in my mother's house.

Seeking some kind of love and stability, I quickly attached myself to some of my teachers. Their kindness helped me see there was always someone there for me, to push me out of a life I could have so easily sunk into. They didn't know it, but there was something about each of those teachers that I wanted to be. Loving, smart, caring, authoritative. Confident.

Teachers aren't just found in school, by the way.

Every person you meet is a teacher. You are a teacher too. Life is learning and everyone has something to learn.

That person you never liked can teach you to identify what it is about them that triggers you.

That person ahead of you in the drive-thru line who paid for your food just schooled you in random acts of kindness.

The person yelling at the cashier is showing you how to check your own patience while also inviting you to be compassionate.

These are the lighthouses. The people you meet along the way who guide you as you navigate this crazy life. Pay attention to the light they throw out. It will help you be a better person, guaranteed.

ARE YOU GRIEVING PROPERLY?

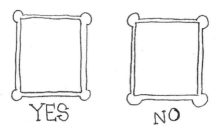

Grief and Guidelines

During readings, people frequently express they feel something is wrong with the way they grieve.

"I'm not grieving the way I'm supposed to."

"Why don't I feel sadder?"

"I thought I would be crying so much more."

We push ourselves to grieve a certain way based on a construct created by others.

Grief presents differently for everyone. The mother whose son passed from a drug overdose told me she said goodbye long before the overdose happened.

A daughter felt empty when her abusive mother died alone in a hospital because she had already grieved the death of hope for a healthy relationship.

Yes, my friends, you can grieve while people are still living.

My office isn't a place for coming to ask Spirit to forgive you for a perceived transgression. You can tell me you want to know that the dead are okay and at peace, but it's really *you* wondering if *you* are okay. When someone dies, it's normal to wonder what we could have done better.

Grief and healing have to happen subconsciously and simultaneously. Death is inevitable—we all know that—but it's grief that will make you show up in your own life.

If you feel regret because you weren't there at the moment of death, you need to push that shit away. You were where you were supposed to be when that death happened. There is nothing you could have done to change the outcome. You have to find peace within yourself. Their death was about them, not about you. And know that while we may have been preparing for the death of a loved one who was ill, so were they. At some point, the dying check out mentally in preparation to transition from this world to the Spirit world. Their energy is already gone. There is nothing you can change.

And honestly, do you really—*really*—want to be there? Which memory do you want to hold on to: the moment of their death or how they were while they were living? Are you trying to make amends? Get closure? Coax out a confession?

Trying to find peace as someone is about to pass is wasted effort. You had plenty of time to have the important conversations when they were alive, and yet you're trying to cram it all in as they are dying. So many of us wait to have the hard conversations because they bring heartbreak. But they also bring the heartbeat back into your life. Talking about the hard stuff brings the blip back from a flatline.

When it comes to grief, guilt and regret are two words that get bounced around on the regular. In grief, it's easy to get caught up in our internal chatter—the coulda, woulda, shoulda. Give these feelings room to be. Acknowledge and recognize them, then stop holding onto them.

You can grieve without bearing the weight of guilt and regret that isn't yours to carry. Show up for yourself. Remind yourself that you don't need to hold on to things you can't change. You need to make room for the things that serve you, bring you joy, and help you find inner peace. Preserve your own mental health and well-being.

If you don't know where to start, let me help. Finish these sentences:

I feel ...

I know ...

I'm aware ...

I allow ...

For example: "I feel like I should be sadder. I know I separated myself from that toxic relationship a long time ago. I'm aware that he was never going to acknowledge the pain he caused me. I allow myself to move forward without regret."

Life is great, but death is profound. It wakes us up for the next chapter. And now you get to choose how to navigate your life. Choose *your* story.

The Last Supper

On March 24, 2021, I asked my cousin in Nova Scotia to go get a donair and a Boston cream donut and take it to my mother for her birthday. Donairs are not only the official food of Halifax, they are one of my mother's favourite foods. Even though our relationship was rocky and tumultuous, it was important to me to try to do the right thing. Even if my mother sucked the joy out of my life, I wasn't going to be the one to suck it out of hers. I would be the bigger person. I could be a good daughter, even if she would never appreciate that. It wasn't an ideal way to celebrate my mom's birthday, but I enjoyed every moment of watching her on video.

She was making yummy noises as she bit into the donair, deeply enjoying the meal. She was using her fingers to pick up the saucy, sweet meat and feed it into her mouth. Every moment of that meal was bliss for both of us in very different ways. She was so caught up in the 20 minutes of joy eating her two favourite foods, that we could both forget for a while that she was bedridden. It was wonderful that I could experience that happiness with her.

I can't remember the last time I had a meal with my mom. I had no idea that this was to be my goodbye meal with her. Three weeks later, she died.

When my mom passed, I called my cousin and asked her to turn the camera so I could see my mother.

"Mama, mama, mama," I repeated as I looked at her lifeless body. It was raw emotion, something I could never have expressed when she was alive. I know, without a doubt, my mother would have thrown this reaction back in my face. But her death had lifted the pressure for me to behave a certain way. It was her final gift to me.

In the months following her death, I realized my grief wasn't about her passing. I was grieving the life I never had with my mother. My mother took secrets about her life—and by extension mine—to the grave. I will probably never know who my father was, nor will I ever understand why my mother chose to never tell me and fill in the missing pieces.

Going forward, my journey of finding out who I really am will be done on my own. The half-truths, lies, and omissions will have to lay as they are, lost forever to me. My relationship with my mother will never be healed, but I can rest easy knowing that I can still have a connection through Spirit, one that will be stronger and healthier for me than how we were in the physical world.

Dirty Dimes

R aise your hand if you've ever found a random dime and thought it was a message from Spirit. How about feathers or butterflies? I always bring this up in my show, wondering aloud how Spirit knew to switch to dimes when Canada phased out pennies. I also wonder why Spirit feels some random dirty coins are an appropriate method for delivering a message. Why not send me a $50 bill? Why not clear my credit card?

I'm not saying this is the wrong message to tune into, though. If finding coins and trinkets helps you move forward or make a hard decision, then so be it. If you are open to receiving signs in nature from your loved ones in the Spirit world, then that's what you will find. Next time you get behind the wheel of your car, think about yellow cars and take note of how many you see. If I tell you not to think about pink elephants, isn't that the first thing that pops into your mind?

Our minds are funny and extremely powerful. They're always working, even while we sleep. I believe each of our minds is connected to Spirit, but some of us are more open to listening than others.

So, sure, you may find dimes that remind you of a loved one. Maybe the coins represent something tangible for you that you are receiving since you no longer have your loved one here. It's your way of holding on somehow. Look at dimes and butterflies as the beginning of you plugging into your awareness. You learn such different things between your spiritual kindergarten and your spiritual Grade 12. If you stop at the beginning of your learning, this is all you will be available for—a kindergarten experience. Before someone close to you passed, were you seeing dimes? If so, what did they mean to you then? Was it just a dirty coin?

Messages can be so rich in meaning. What the dime or butterfly is showing you is what it is like to be present and to be connected to more than just random things that drift into our sightlines.

Spirit would like you to want more of a connection to energy than dirty coins on the ground. Would you be okay with that?

Finding change can be your sign to start making change. Start searching for more.

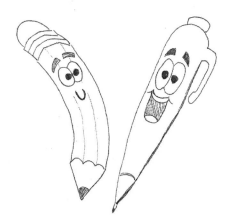

Be the Pencil

When you write the story of your life, are you jotting it down with a pencil or pen?

A pencil is a safe option, because most pencils come with an eraser. A friend of mine never uses a pencil when she does crosswords. That bitch commits. She is so confident she knows the answers, she only uses pen.

But pencil lead is erasable for a reason: It gives you a chance to learn and to expand your lesson. You are allowed to make mistakes, rub them away, and create something better. This theory applies to life just as much as it applies to school (and okay, maybe not so much to crossword puzzles and their "only one right answer." Stupid things.).

How do you want to write (or re-write) your story? Using a pencil and eraser leaves lots of room to change something if you don't like it. Lead and rubber allow you to make a choice and exert your free will. You have the ability to correct your mistakes and learn from them. If you are not sharpened by your experiences, like a pencil, you will become blunt and stunted.

A pen is somewhat more permanent. It means you fully intend to follow through, but it can also limit your options for growth. Change your mind, and you'll make a mess scratching out what you just put down.

You can cover up your mistakes, but they will never be completely gone, even when the ink runs dry.

Figure out where you are in your life right now and choose your instrument. The nice thing about being a human being is we can fuck up and fix our mistakes. Go back to the pencil if you need a do-over.

However, don't be one of those people who chooses the permanent marker option. It's indelible—not able to be forgotten or removed. So many people I encounter are on this path, repeating harmful behaviours, with no desire or drive to change their path. I get that it's easy for me to hide behind a keyboard and tell you to leave an abusive relationship, but actually doing it takes more guts than maybe you have right now.

It's okay. You'll be okay. Whichever instrument you use, learn from your mistakes and own them.

Jennie's Gems

GRIEF WIPES EVERYTHING OFF YOUR WHITEBOARD.
IT REARRANGES YOUR ALPHABET. IT FUCKS WITH
EVERYTHING.

Screaming out the Grief

2020 was supposed to be my year. As 2019 came to a close, I was riding on the wave of all my hard work over the years. I had made so many sacrifices, run shows and readings back-to-back, hit the road for trips, and consumed more roadside coffee and hotel buffet pancakes than any doctor would advise, but I was moving forward in my career.

And then, in March 2020 life unravelled. I lost everything I never had and it hurt. I was working with a production company in Los Angeles to develop a television series, but COVID brought all production to a full stop; I lost an opportunity for a TV pilot with Slice and TLC. My live shows and in-person readings could not happen at all. Overnight, I lost all my income and all my light.

I grieved the loss of something I never had. My expectations for 2020 were sky high. They were so large they created a hole when my life did not meet those expectations. I was so deep in wishing and hoping for these amazing things, it never occurred to me that I wouldn't have them.

I let myself sit in shock and sadness for a while. I drove out of the city, finding myself next to an empty field. I got out of my car and screamed. I screamed out all my hurt and disappointment. And you know what?

It felt good. It felt like a storm cloud finally letting loose after hours of rumbling clouds. Sweet, sweet, relief.

Give yourself permission to scream and let everything out. Scream into a pillow if that works for you. Release. Mourn. Get pissed off. Then scream your fucking head off. Then, and only then, can you change your perspective. When I was done screaming my throat raw, I realized all the things I lost were never mine to begin with and were not meant to be.

Scream until you're empty and you know you are done. Releasing grief creates room for better things in your life.

Whispering

For the longest time, I could never—would never—share out loud what I was capable of doing. I was surrounded by people whispering, wondering who my father was, what I was going to do next, how badly my mother abused me. Needless to say, I was not a fan of whispers. It's kind of ironic that Spirit now whispers in my ear.

I've never understood why people whisper serious disease or mental health issues, like speaking them aloud makes them contagious. You won't get cancer by acknowledging it. You won't be inclined to take your own life if you talk about suicide. Even in a whisper, you are still making noise.

But I've come to appreciate that not all whispering is harmful.

We need to make noise in our lives. If you speak your truth, sure, you'll piss off some people. Trust me, I have *lots* of experience in this department. I don't live life quietly. Never have, never will.

People visiting the graves of their loved ones will engage in a whispered one-way conversation. Prayers for guidance or strength are whispered in the dark. When was the last time you whispered the name of your loved one as you reached out for an embrace?

And every damn day, your own gut is whispering

to you. Your instincts are guiding you, telling you when something feels very right or terribly wrong. Listen to the whispers. Life is bigger than just physical sensations. There is an infinity to awareness, to knowing. Listen to the whispers.

Be Your Own Hero

Once upon a time, there was a girl, a non-princess, the child of an abusive mother who beat her and got rid of her every weekend she could. Dad was a mystery and Mom was not emotionally invested. There was no king or queen or glorious kingdom.

What the hell kind of fairy tale is that?

As children, we believed in the tale of Cinderella and all the other storybooks we grew up on. It becomes a goal for many little girls to find their Prince Charming. Fairy tales are all lies, exclusionary and with zero foundation in real life. Still, most parents read them to their children, and even if we take the time to point out that maybe Cinderella likes girls or Prince Charming might want to wear the glass slipper himself, we perpetuate the myths.

So much so that even when we fail to reach a fairy-tale ending of our own, we hold on to the idea of the fairy tale. In some cases, the unrealistic version of life we read about or see in the movies becomes the best-case scenario.

Can anyone ever find a realistic example of a fairy tale?

Does the non-princess have a chance at becoming Cinderella or will she end up washing floors for her whole life?

She's not good with a mop, but she's been really good at cleaning up her own shit. Taking the first steps to control your own life is not easy, but it really is worth the work.

Think about your own personal Cinderella story and tell yourself you are entitled to your own version of the glass slipper. Drop the mop and step into the custom pumps.

All Readings Have Potential

There's no such thing as a good or bad reading for me. Each time someone sits in front of me or when I step out into an audience, there are a thousand things that have to happen. So many things have to align in the moment. I have to be ready to channel and the people have to be ready to receive. I have to clear the way for Spirit to come through. I need to push aside any nervous energy—mine or theirs. Spirit needs to work with me, not against me, giving me signs that I can understand.

I once was sitting with a message circle of 15 people who came together for readings. Among the group were a mother and daughter. The daughter's energy was poking at me like a tack.

"Why are you looking at me like that?" I asked her. "You're looking at me like you're analyzing me." She was indeed. She was a therapist.

I brought through the mother's mother-in-law, but the messages I was receiving were weird and convoluted.

"I have to pull back," I told the mom and daughter. "Everything is disjointed and cloudy. I can't see where I'm going. Nothing is making sense."

I moved on to other readings, but I was repeatedly being pulled back to them. There was something Spirit wanted them to know, but the mother and daughter were throwing energetic blocks in my way.

Upon further discussion, I discovered they were both hoping I would channel their son/brother who died a decade ago, but he was not coming through.

"I'm getting nothing. I don't feel I'm supposed to channel him today," I told them.

The daughter's eyes drifted away from me, then back again.

"I'm disappointed," she said.

"Why?" I asked.

"It'd be kind of nice to hear from him," she answered, teary-eyed.

"But wait a minute. You came here expecting that your brother would come, but your energy is in a totally different place and not available. I gotta be honest, me channelling your brother isn't going to bring you peace today."

I told her she didn't need to hear from her brother, and she needed to let go of compartmentalizing her life. The daughter found me fascinating and was so busy trying to figure me out that she was not present in the moment.

People often want me to prove myself to them with some kind of parlour trick, like pulling fairy dust or unicorns out of my ass. Or by calling a specific Spirit to appear to me on demand. I can't, won't, and don't do that.

I have to sit back and see the energy of everyone

involved. You know exactly what I'm talking about if you've ever walked into a room and felt a vibe. That's the energy of the space.

A tough reading happens when someone is not open. It's hard work getting someone to open up, to be accepting of the information Spirit is asking me to share. It's like I'm facing a wall with not a single loose brick. A challenging reading becomes like Spirit Pictionary, with me presenting a person with every-thing laid out in front of them, but they can't put the pieces together. While I hate quitting, I have to remain open to discontinuing a difficult session, acknowl-edging some people are not ready for someone like me.

With readings that flow, I can feel the energy in the room. It's palpable. The energy changes in my body. Messages are quick and bright. There's laughter and tears. And lots of revelations. At the end of an enriching reading, everyone feels full, relaxed, and satisfied, like they have just had the best Spiritual meal of their life.

And then there are the readings when I am faced with someone whose arms are crossed in front of their chest. Their lips are pursed, their eyes squinting. Their body language is screaming, "This is such phony bullshit."

This happened in a group reading, where a dozen people sat around a table in a hotel conference room. These people were a mix of family members and long-time friends. They knew each other deeply and had been together through a series of life events, some that were very tragic. I sat at the head of the table.

To my right sat a mother, father, daughter, and cousin. At the other end of the table, a husband and wife who were friends with all of the others. To my left, another mother and two of her three daughters. The mother's lips were pressed together in judgment.

Spirit checked in with me, bringing messages for the people on the right. Tears were shed, but still, the mother on my left was not believing. More than an hour into the reading, a message came through for her.

"You were married three times," I said to her.

"I was," she nodded.

"And you were very loved by all three."

She shrugged, then looked down at her hands resting in her lap.

"They're all together in Spirit world, you know. Husband number two wants you to know he still enjoys the sound of your laugh. The one that catches you by surprise. It's different from your other laughter."

"That's true, Mom," one of her daughters said.

"It's true of most people," the mom countered. "You could say that about anybody."

I heard her, but I was still listening to her second husband who was showing me something interesting.

"Hang on," I said, looking over to a blank space on the wall. I was reading the signs being shown to me, and I wasn't sure how to interpret them. *What are you trying to say?* But the image was holding steady, so I went with it.

"Did you just buy a new bra?" I asked the woman. "Like, a fancy one ... black lace?"

Her face reddened. "Come on," she gasped, clasping her hands in front of her chest. "How can you possibly know that?"

"Husband number 2 showed me," I answered. "They all like it, by the way," I winked.

From that point, the three-time widow was all in. I had even more validations for her: that I knew she was in the car with her third husband when they were hit by a drunk driver, and that he died in that car. It feels great when I can open up a tough client.

However a reading goes, I know this for sure: in order for a reading to flow, the energy has to be open and positive. Park your expectations at the door, because mediums have no control and if they tell you they do, run. You might not get what you want from me, but you'll get what you need.

The All-You-Can-Eat Chinese Buffet

I f you don't like hitting up an all-you-can-eat Chinese buffet, I'm sorry, but we can't be friends. I'm joking, obviously. But for real, how can you not like a buffet? Even after the pandemic, I can't resist the lure of chicken balls and ginger beef.

Every time I make plans to go to a Chinese food buffet, I pre-starve myself, only out of a sense of value. I want to get the most bang for my buck. I want to leave knowing I ate $34.99 worth of chicken balls, pork fried rice, and ginger beef. Don't judge. Y'all know you've done the same thing (remember that open bar, Susan?).

The foods may vary at different buffets, but how we behave is exactly the same. We get the white plate, beeline for the things we love and pile on. The first heaping is pretty big, because a) we are hungry and b) we have the freedom to do so.

Even before we sit down to eat, we are planning what we will get on our second visit. As we loaded the plate, we were side-eyeing the dessert bank, assessing the offerings like a rancher at a roadhouse.

And the next time you go, it will be exactly the same, from the food to the experience. The buffet is reliable for its abundance and its familiarity. But imagine if someone stopped you and sliced half the things off your plate, replacing it with something terrible, like eggplant Parmesan. What would you do?

Would you eat it? Would you hit the bastard upside of the head with a slab of roast beef?

I'm here to tell you to take the risk and taste the damn eggplant. You might really like it. Imagine that. Doing something unfamiliar and out of *your* ordinary can be a positive experience.

When you only taste the dishes you've had before, you are only filling your plate with the familiar. There is no room for improvement. You are passing up the opportunity to cleanse your palate with something new and exciting.

When you keep going back for more of the same, you can never know the possibilities. Sometimes, you have to let someone else choose what to put on your plate and blindly follow that path. It's what helps us grow and discover new things about ourselves.

I'd never consciously line up for eggplant Parmesan and pass on the beef and broccoli or ginger beef. I'd remain open to giving it a try (which I have, and no, I do not like eggplant parm). Life is way too short to fill your plate with the same stuff over and over. Clear your plate of the things that no longer serve you. Fill your plate with joy.

Jennie's Gems

GROWTH REQUIRES FIGHTING TWO DEMONS: EXPECTATIONS AND EXPERIENCE.

The Fuck Sandwich

The fuck sandwich is filled with all the shit you won't—or can't—deal with. This sandwich is the place in life where all the crap causing you pain is spread between two soggy slices of bullshit bread.

When you find yourself seated in front of a fuck sandwich, you are stuck in a place of regret. It's a miserable place to be. A fuck sandwich is most commonly served at a picnic full of people who are filled with bitterness, guilt, and shame. Which means those are the kinds of people you end up surrounded by.

Because misery loves company. Everyone makes fuck sandwiches, but we all use different ingredients.

The next time you feel helpless, frozen, or just plain tired of being miserable, find the will to fight. Claw your way out of the middle of that fuck sandwich and find a Danish or some other delicious pastry. That's where you deserve to be.

Bitch Jennie

We all have a bitch inside. You may not call her your inner bitch. She might be mean, sarcastic, or just really damn tired. But she's in there. For the purposes of getting my point across, she's the bitch.

The bitch self stands up for herself. She forms a protective wall to keep others at a distance. She comes from a place of pain, avoiding dealing with things, and not processing. Bitch energy will never be objective. It is wholly and unapologetically coming from within. When you build a wall, you think you are keeping people out, but what you're really doing is keeping yourself in.

It was through my mother's passing that I realized Bitch Jennie was usually in control when it came to that relationship. It was the wall I hid behind to navigate my way through the pain and disappointment. I was relieved when my mother died. It meant that the 47-year chapter of hell for me was now over. While I sat thinking about the path of my life without my mother, I was now free to start working on the things that really mattered. The work would be complicated, like taking apart an emotional clock to see how things worked.

Bitch Jennie was glad Mom died because she couldn't hurt her anymore. Mom's energy couldn't suck life from real Jennie and real Jennie could now open her heart and start to heal. I was starting to feel something different. A piece of my heart that had never been opened was beating to life. My life was now my own, not something tainted by my mom.

Bitch Jennie allowed me to create boundaries, but necessarily healthy ones. Now that my mother is gone, I can stop trying to figure out how to be a better daughter. Instead, I can now allow myself to indulge in self-care for real Jennie only.

When the bitch moves aside, you can start caring about caring for yourself, FINALLY!

S.H.O.W. M.E.

I never thought I'd be someone who would get in my car and drive, without a plan, without a hotel booked, without a passenger in the seat next to me keeping me company. But now that I've done that (more than once), I crave this solitude. I gift myself this chance to be quiet. I sit in silence and think about who I am, who I was, and where I am going. Mulling over shit from the past isn't just about healing, it's also about learning lessons. I don't need to justify anything from the past, but I need to examine the patterns that have perpetuated in my life.

Almost a decade ago, in the early days of my work, I felt like I was off-centre in what I was doing, lost and lonely in being a medium. I knew I was on the right path, but I still asked for a sign of confirmation. It was a crisp January night when I walked out onto the patio behind my house, and looked up to the sky to see a double shooting star.

I heard a whisper say, "Show Me." I didn't interpret this as having to prove myself to anyone. I understood "Show Me" to mean a way of living life. Each letter stood for something that could guide me to live authentically, to feel comfortable with my path, and to trust the future ahead of me would be of my own making.

I was led to break the words up into an acronym that was easy to recall:

S: Shut up and listen
H: Handcraft your experience
O: OMG moment
W: Why are you doing this?

M: Magnificent, manifesting, magical
E: Excellent, exploring, exceptional

If I committed to live with the S.H.O.W., then I could easily define the M.E.

Following this acronym as a process will drive you to be a human being, moving you away from the busy work of a human doing. Here's how the process can work.

Shut Up and Listen: Savour the quiet. Stop worrying about the next thing you want to say. When someone is cutting you down, listen to what they are telling you about themselves, their own insecurities, and their fears. It will change your relationships when you start hearing what is really being said. Pay attention to the lesson.

Handcraft Your Experience: Are you doing the things you want to do in life or are you just keeping the peace? Examine your life like Spirit would: from afar and out of body. If you could change one thing about your day today, what would you do differently? Hand-crafting your experience won't happen overnight. It's a long journey, but once you start, you can make it a habit.

OMG Moment: This moment happens when things light up, when you have extreme clarity about what's not working in life and you know how to change it.

Why Are You Doing This?: Before you embark on any major changes, you need to have a deep under-standing of your motivation. Are you doing this for you or to make someone else love you more? It's hard to separate your own true needs from those driven by a lifetime of trying to live up to someone else's expecta-tions. One way to answer this question is to pause before you act. This will help you determine if you are moving in the right direction.

The "M.E." can stand for whatever you want, but it has to be something that has meaning for you. Your "M.E." is looking within yourself for inspiration, not leaving it to outside sources. Pick the words corre-sponding to those letters that have meaning for you. They should be positive and/or words of action.

"M" can be mentorship, meditation, or massage. Musical, muscular, or mellifluous.

"E" can represent excitement, experience, or ebul-lience. Evangelical, eager, empowered.

It was when I had nailed my own "S.H.O.W. M.E.," that I decided to become 100 percent Jennie and do the work to make my life better. I taught myself to stop giving a shit about a lot of things and to live without a filter. It's so freeing to move forward without tip-toeing around everyone else. If someone doesn't like how you are, they can leave the fucking room.

Doing the work means figuring out how you do you. Get to know yourself and pay attention to your energy, understand what lights you up, and what brings you down. Figure yourself out, handcraft your identity, take control of the internal conversation. Because I am confident in who I am, I can walk into any situation and find my footing. You can, too.

Heartbreaker

I never believed anyone could love me. The people who were supposed to love me taught me to believe that I wasn't worthy, and this was why I tended to keep people at arm's length. Until I learned that people would love me for who I was, I would typically leave a relationship before I could get hurt. It became the pattern in my life to leave, not giving them the chance to leave me first.

Because I was never fully invested in my relationships, I got bored very quickly. This was a reflection on me, not my partner. I never allowed myself to enjoy the adventure of a new love. I refused to let someone else do the driving, and this led to an imbalance where I was taking more than I was capable of giving. I never meant to hurt anybody, it's just that I'm a heartbreaker. I was the one to end all my relationships. I had to figure out that love didn't equate to sex.

Basic love is like a bungalow. It's safe and even. You settle down, share bills, divide the housework.

Great love is a high rise. It's exciting and lofty. You focus on creating a life with the people who are living in it.

Sure, if you fall from a high rise, it's a longer, harder, more painful fall than tripping out the front door of a bungalow. But holy, the view is so much better.

Relinquishing Control

Claudia came into my office with the burden of death hanging heavy around her. Her mother had passed away four months previously and she could not get over the loss.

The day before her mother's death was a day filled with joy. They went shopping together. They had a lovely lunch. Claudia dropped her mom off at home and went back to her own house. The next day, her mom was going to come over to babysit Claudia's three-year-old daughter.

Mom never made it. She passed away, alone, in her own home.

"I don't get it," Claudia said to me through her tears. "I *just* saw her."

"Death doesn't get to be scheduled," I explained. "Your mother died without pain. Isn't that something you wanted for her?"

Over and over, we hear stories of people passing in horrible ways. A fatal car accident. Death at the hands of an abusive partner. Months or years of suffering from an incurable disease.

"Would you choose to watch her lose weight, lose strength, lose her appetite, slowly fading to nothing? Would you choose that because you could see it coming?"

Of course, the answer is no. Going peacefully is always preferred.

Claudia was overwhelmed and filled with anxiety. And that beast we all know: regret. She never had her chance to say goodbye.

"One more time telling someone you love them won't change the fact that they died," I told her.

For Claudia, her journey with me helped her unearth what the real issue was. As a strong, confident woman, she was having a hard time accepting something she couldn't control. She admitted she dwells on things, especially when they don't work out exactly the way she wanted them to.

Death has this tricky way of bringing up the dirt in our lives. It can reopen our emotional scars. Don't wait for someone else's death to help you recognize where you need to do your work. Deal with the real problems now. Peel off the wallpaper hiding your pain. Underneath, I'm sure you can find your joy.

Being a Mom and a Medium

When my daughter was younger, she asked for my business card to hand out at school and then she would tell me when her teachers were going to come to my shows. While that's cool, and all her friends know what I do, I know I'm a bit different from the other moms she knows.

She has a gay mom who talks to dead people.

On the plus side, I get to use the Spirit card to remind her to be truthful. She cannot lie. She can't hide anything from me. Mom's intuition, Spirit snitches, same thing.

But... I'll never be on the list of entrepreneurs asked to share their experience during Career Day at the Catholic school.

Doing My Own Work

It's part of my job to help people see the light. I give my clients unsolicited advice. I tell them the things they don't want to hear. I never make anything easy.

It's incredibly hard to turn the focus inward, to examine where I've set my limitations. I tell people to be open-minded, but for a long time, I kept my own mind closed to the opportunities life offers.

I've spent a lot of my life alone. I've pushed people away. My childhood wasn't rewarding nor safe. Now that I am older, I am changing my perspective. What I couldn't control—the abuse, the abandonment—shouldn't be kept in my front pocket. I allowed myself to carry this pain for a long time. I need to let it go. I am strong enough to process that and learn from it.

Everyone is going to have someone die, and that will bring up all the emotions around that person that you didn't deal with when they were alive. It's exhausting.

Death is the catalyst that sends you to the point where you need to be invested in your life.

In all this work, I am finding my path too. I am doing my own work.

Jennie's Gems

WHAT DEATH MAKES US DO is adjust our lens on
life.

This Thing Called Life

As a mother, I have a duty to prepare my daughter for all the things life will throw at her. There will be great things and hurtful things, scary things and loving things.

Life isn't always about extremes. Not every experience has to be life-changing in order to have value. Every damn day that you show up is worth celebrating.

I tell my daughter every day that I love her and point out what makes her fascinating. I tell her that she is a good human. I instill in her all the important qualities that make her "be." I want her to get the most out of this crazy thing we call life.

I try to do the same thing every time I do a reading. I want to inspire everyone to do better, be stronger, and embrace the gift of awareness that death can give us.

Every day we get to create something. If everyone woke up and had to be invested in their life for at least 20 minutes a day by creating something new or looking for a new opportunity instead of waiting for it to come to them, no one would spend time sitting around wondering why their life is so shitty.

Move your life forward by understanding what you are no longer going to do. Step into the dream of where you are going, where you can go, where you want to go. Stop obsessing about what you don't have or where you failed. Move the starting line so you can be closer to where you want to finish.

Where I Go Before the Show

In the early days of my career as a medium, I felt I needed to light a candle before I started channelling. I put my mind into the right flow for a show.

With the candlelight flickering, I would visualize an escalator. I would take it to the top and land on an giant-sized air hockey table. Waiting for me on the table were a big push broom and a little broom, inviting me to sweep a path from Jennie's world through to Spirit world. With the big broom, I brushed my way through the dust and then I set it down. I got the little broom to sweep the path clear of the little bits and pieces until a pebble path appeared on the air hockey table. I could feel the little stones under my toes. I kept walking until the pebbles disappeared and there, at the end of the table, saloon doors appeared. Once they swung open, my Spirit guide was there.

"Are you ready to work?" it asked.

I'd nod. "Okay, we're going in. So get those people lined up for me."

That's when I'm ready to work.

If you think I'm floating on a cloud or sitting with a wise man on a mountain, there is none of that. I'm on an escalator and an air hockey table.

Where I Go After the Show

Once the show is done and the hall or bar or restaurant has cleared, I know I can release. As soon as the show is over, my brain releases my body. Once I say, "Thank you and have a good night," I close down.

And then I fart for probably half an hour.

The Gift

When someone refers to what I do as a gift, it always sounds like a Hallmark movie to me.

I always knew I was different, but I didn't know that my version of "different" was so vastly different from what everyone else could or couldn't do. I still think it's weird that other people can't sense this energy.

Yet I did what everyone else did. I went out and found a job, did the nine to five, and I got caught up in all of that. But I always knew there was something different for me. I was never a good employee. I had way too many things to say and boundaries have always been an issue for me.

When I finally started working as a medium, it was amazing. I finally could put my voice behind the things that I knew.

I had to do a lot of personal work to understand that this information wasn't mine. Messages from Spirit are not mine to filter, they're mine to give.

All the people I get to sit with and be a part of their healing and their journey—what better job is there than that?

My first real big show happened in Cochrane, Alberta. I had no idea what I was going to do, but I woke up one day and out of the blue a voice said, "You need to do shows." At the time, I had no idea where this voice came from or who it was. It was my first experience with my Spirit guide. I didn't question it. Instead, I found a way to make it happen. Two hundred and forty-five people came to that first show.

I enjoy standing up in front of a large group of people and channelling for two hours. I love giving people a new perspective on death. My purpose is not to change your opinion. I'm simply here to share what I know. The rest is up to you.

Why Spirit Shows Up

From the minute I walked into the arena, the loss overwhelmed me. From every curve of the boards in the now-defrosted hockey rink, I felt the sorrow of every mother in the space. It caught me by surprise, but I should have anticipated this. When I was invited to do readings at a special Mother's Day lunch at a First Nations community in central Alberta, I suspected the energy would be vibrant. In my mind, a deeply spiritual culture would throw the doors to Spirit wide open, and the messages would flow.

As soon as I stood among the women seated in the rink, I had a flash of a young man dead behind a house. When I scanned the vision, I could see under the house, which was weird. I sensed this death was an accidental overdose because I was feeling and smelling drugs in the body. I can't explain it, but I just knew.

I called out to the crowd, asking who had a connection to someone who had passed under a house. A lady stood up and said her son died from an accidental overdose. He was found under an abandoned house that sat on raised stilts. I asked her about a black jean jacket with painting on the back and her eyes welled up.

"He wore that jacket everywhere," she choked, "even when it was summer."

It's pretty phenomenal to me when I can help people with those validations.

I hope that in the few minutes I worked with her, she found some peace. After all the times she woke up and didn't feel her son with her, she felt him in those few minutes. I hope that it changed her for the better, knowing that she is still connected to her son.

When I work with a mother who has experienced such trauma, week after week, I need to separate from it or it will harm me permanently. When I work with Spirit, I create a bubble that is separate from my own being. It gives me distance from medium Jennie. I've saved space for Jennie—the mom, the friend, the partner.

People come to my shows because it's uplifting. I look at things differently. I say "fuck" a lot. I can lift up the people in the room with the energy all coming together. We laugh as much as we cry

There's this idea that Spirit is smarter than you, but I don't see it that way. They don't have all the answers. They don't show up to focus on their death. They come out of love. They don't want to take you back to that moment of death or pain. They come to help transition the living, to help facilitate your evolution of self.

Spirit's job isn't to answer the hard questions, their job is to support you in the decisions that you make. People who have crossed don't come back to remind you that they're dead, they come back to remind you that you have a life to live. They come through because they have something to tell you or they see something going on in your life that requires their support.

My job as the reader is to pass on the message without too much interpretation, but I have to push people out of their comfort zones. If you stay in your safe place, there is no space for amazing things to happen. You can't collide with interesting things or people in life if you never stray out of your comfort zone.

In a show, I limit what I share from Spirit. I'm not going to call you out in front of 150 people. That's what a private reading is for. In private, I can share my energy with one person for the entire session. It gives me the opportunity to be more detailed and more intricate. But don't ask me to ask Spirit for the answers on how to improve your life.

Spirit has way more important things to do than help you find your keys.

The Things We Can't Touch

Your mind is where all your intangibles sit.
    Your trust.
    Your love, passion, and desires.
Your purpose.

Your intent, honesty, and bravery.

What we live our lives by is something we cannot even physically hold. We can only experience.

So why are we always chasing *stuff*?

Jennie's Gems

BE THE EXPERT IN YOUR OWN LIFE. IT'S YOUR JOB TO WRITE YOUR ADVENTURE.

Party On

We celebrate all the milestones: birthdays, weddings, anniversaries, retirements. We plan these events down to the last detail. Before a woman is married or a baby is even born, we throw a shower.

Someone who has a terminal illness *should* have a parting party. I think we should have death showers. None of us are getting out of here alive, so why wouldn't we want to plan one of our biggest days ahead? Celebrate while you can be here. Face things instead of skirting them.

Sharing the moments of life is empowering. It can help you embrace death. You can face your end on your own terms. As a side bonus, you'll leave your loved ones with memories of how you went out strong and maybe with a beer in your hand.

It's not morbid to plan for, celebrate, and acknowledge death. To me, stuffing a dead animal full of crap and hanging it on a wall is morbid. I could handle that better when I thought taxidermy was bumper cars for cabs.

After you die, everyone you know can get hammered, but why shouldn't they do that while you are here and can reminisce with your loved ones and watch them get stupid drunk? Isn't that more fun than having a collection of sombre faces crowding around your death bed?

I picture my own death shower as a weekend gathering of all the important people in my life, sharing memories and laughing our asses off about the crazy things we did. We'd have deep conversations about how we all contributed to one another's lives. It would be an opportunity for others to tell me how they contributed to my legacy in an open, loving, and caring way.

And if you are one of the lucky ones who beats the odds and lives past the doctor-issued death sentence, celebrate the fuck out of that.

Feeling Lost

Feeling lost is not a bad place to be. It's not a dead end or a vacuum where all your life purpose gets sucked away. When people feel lost, there's a reason they go someplace to find themselves.

Feeling lost can happen at any time in our lives. That empty feeling might strike when we lose a job or when someone we love dies or when we are on the edge of a midlife crisis. This sense of not knowing what's next is something everyone experiences at one point or another.

When we feel lost, it's because we are about to change, morph, and grow. Being lost means you are ready to step out of your comfort zone, face fear, and follow a passion.

It happened to me when I quit my nine-to-five job, opting instead to work with Spirit for one year. I chose to say "yes" to my heart's desire, but within a time limit. I wish I could say I flourished during that year, but it was hard. I was a single mom with a five-year-old. I gave up stability. But even when I walked away from the security, I tried to put limits on what I was willing to do. Doing readings publicly was a risk I wasn't ready to take. I wasn't ready to put myself on display, preferring instead the intimacy of a private reading with a person who was 100 percent convinced that Spirit was real. I was still trying to exercise control and doing that 100 percent limited my experience. In my head, I had ideas of how the year should look, what should happen, and what I should get out of life. I was "shoulding" all over myself.

At the time, I didn't know that trying to act a certain way, a way that wasn't genuine to me, meant I was still going to feel lost at the end of my year. Stability would come from honouring myself and letting myself be free. Sure, I'd be broke and hungry some of the time, but feeling lost can happen on a full stomach as well.

You have to trust your gut without setting limits. Jumping in is always an option, because trying to fit your dreams into a "If I do this, then that has to happen" box is a shitty place to try to make a life. Focus more on the journey than the destination. Know where you're going, even if you don't know how to get there.

I'd rather be lost on the path to my dream than found someplace I don't want to be. I'd much rather be trying to figure out how I can live my true purpose than be stuck in a nine-to-five job that I hate. To me, that is truly where we get lost.

Finding Myself in the Middle of Nowhere

I've felt lost plenty of times in my life. One summer, I felt driven to get intentionally lost. My daughter was spending a month travelling with my ex-wife, and I was restless. Everyone thought I was crazy to set off in my car, alone, with the intent of driving anywhere. I had no definite destination. I had planned to drive in whatever direction I pleased. I brought what I needed to transform the back of my car into a home on wheels. I had my clothes, water, food, a mattress, and a sleeping bag. My plan was simple: stay off the main roads and always camp near water.

I wanted to be with me, my intuition, and let myself be guided wherever I was supposed to go. It was to be a trip of taking risks and just being.

For three weeks, I took care of just me. I dunked myself in sketchy rivers and bathed in Walmart parking lots. Being alone, often without cell service, gave me the opportunity to crawl inside my own head.

Without distractions, I could put energy into journaling, a practice I wholeheartedly believe in. Writing things down as my mind wanders gives power to my dreams. It gives me a record of where I was, mentally, in that exact moment. In my journal, I can list the things that really matter; I can pin down the ideas swirling in my head.

Several times, I found myself sitting at the edge of a

creek, fully present in the moment and the movement of the water. My fear of being a woman alone evaporated and I let myself get lost in the moment of pure centredness. I felt a shift within me.

I met the most fascinating people on that trip, other travellers on different voyages. As a social person, isolation was hard for me. When I met others, I had pent-up energy and that spilled over into enthusiastic conversations.

Because I did not have to worry about where I was going, this solo trip allowed me to reflect on who I was and what I was doing. If I don't permit myself to do the things I loved, then I was not being who I truly am.

Try it sometime.

When you find yourself in the middle of nowhere, you will find yourself.

The Meaning of a Metaphor

Do you remember the first time you got butterflies in your stomach? How about what gives you goosebumps?

You don't actually have butterflies flapping around and you don't have goose feathers growing from your arms. We use these metaphors because it's so hard to explain these feelings. Goosebumps and butterflies are visceral responses—deep inward feelings—to being present.

I see people rubbing their arms all the time at my shows. I know who's checked out or not involved in what is happening because the latter audience members have no visceral reaction to what is happening around them. You won't feel the tension of a horror movie if you are absorbed in something on your phone.

What does it mean to be present? It's being able to put a finger on a feeling—what passion or love or fear or excitement feels like on a visceral level. It's reactionary and uncontrolled, like those first few moments after a car accident. It's what it can feel like when someone you love dies.

So how do we start working on moving forward after loss? You have to take the time to place yourself before you can put a finger on the feeling. Centre yourself. Ground yourself. Take a moment to expand on the visceral experience by putting words to your emotions.

For example, how does discomfort feel to you? Viscerally, we might feel like we can't sit still or are jittery. If you had to explain it to someone, you need to find the right descriptor, like your skin is too tight, or your shoes are squeezing your toes. Attaching a metaphor gives voice to our emotions, and that, my friend, is what makes you present in your pain. Only once you are present can you move forward from the pain.

Metaphors are ubiquitous in our lives. We use them to communicate with our doctor when we need to explain back pain that is a nail driving into our spine. We use them to describe the weather (pissing rain or blistering heat), our working life (my office is a prison), and the people we love (she is the light of my life). They can also be used to explore our relationship with death.

A lot of what we feel viscerally about death is affected by dialogue. If you change "anxiety" to "excitement," your experience will change. Similarly, if you open the conversation about death, it becomes less taboo. We can prepare ourselves and our loved ones. Have open discussions about what you want in death. Use family dinners to talk about legacies and experiences that have shaped who you are.

Not everyone reacts to death the same way. Some people shut down, while some people take action. Look inward, talk about death, and learn how to be open about the topic. Find new metaphors that will open your emotional doors and allow you to move forward. Instead of viewing death as the final sunset, think of it as moving into a new energy. Don't focus on the long-term loss. Celebrate the chance you had to be part of someone's life. Even if they never told you so, you made a difference for your loved one while they were on Earth.

Jennie's Gems

You can't take out an IOU on your future.
Get your shit done now. Your life is not a
bar tab.

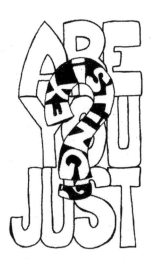

Are You Just Existing?

As soon as my foot hit the first step leading into the house, I saw him. He was a young man, his face partially hidden by the mask and tubes of a ventilator. Before I even rang the doorbell for this appointment, I knew this Spirit was here for the woman I was about to meet.

Once I was in the door, I was distracted by her dogs, and of course I leaned over to pet and play with them. The woman was very gracious, offering me water and a snack. We moved into the living room and I felt the pressing need to tell her what I saw.

"When I was coming up the stairs, I saw a young man on a ventilator. Do you know who that is?"

Her face paled and she fell into a chair.

"How do you know about that?" she gasped. "I thought you just channel dead people?"

"No," I explained, "I channel energy. And I can tell you that this person's energy is already in Spirit world, not behind the mask of the ventilator."

She remained silent, looking at her hands resting in her lap.

"He's showing me the letters, M-U-M. He's telling me to say hi to you. His mum."

"Oh my God," she whispered.

She proceeded to tell me her son had attempted

suicide by taking pills. He was now brain dead and had been for several years. She visits him in the hospital every day.

"Your son's energy is in the Spirit world," I told her, trying to ease her confusion. "He's telling me that he's sorry, but he didn't want to be in this world anymore. He wants you to know that even though you can see his physical body, he's not in it."

She was not prepared to hear from someone she believed was still alive. She wanted me to connect her to her mother. But her son was the one who came through, hoping to help his mum let go and process his physical body's death.

There were more validations coming for this woman. Her son told me his friend came to visit his physical body that morning. He told me that in that moment, he was with his grandmother—the person my client had expected to connect with today. And he explained that though his grandmother suffered through cancer, she was now at ease in the Spirit world. Then he showed me the collection of toys that his mother was saving.

"I saved them because I thought it would help me connect with him," she sighed.

"You don't need that," I said. "You don't need that shoebox of crap. Your son is with you. He's not at the hospital. He's not there. He's right here," I explained, waving my arms over my head.

And there began the road to healing. I can give you confirmation that it's okay to move on. I gave this mum a way to stop existing in the pain of her lost son. I wanted her to know his Spirit was everywhere, waiting for her to acknowledge him.

I experienced a similar situation with a family whose daughter died at a young age due to complications stemming from cerebral palsy.

The parents had so much guilt, believing they could have done something more to keep their daughter alive. I wasn't channelling at the time, but the daughter came through anyway. She had a message she wanted me to deliver. She kept coming to me, prodding me like a rancher moving a calf to pasture.

"What the fuck?" I screamed into the air. "I'm not working!"

But she was relentless.

She was whispering in my ear, telling me that her parents put all of their love into her and now that she was gone, they didn't know where to put that love. Her father was trying to put his love into her mom, and her mom was putting her love into the dog.

"They are not coping," she said.

I took this message to her parents, filling them in on what their daughter was observing.

"You guys are not connecting," I said. "You are only existing together."

After so many readings with so many different

people, I know some people won't give up the grief to make space for the healing. You need to live your life without your loved one. Life is not over for you. It's crucial that you find a way to move on. Doing anything else is just wasting time.

Where I Go Before the Show: Part 2

On a summer trip home to Nova Scotia, I felt pulled to drive down a road I had never travelled before. At the end of the road, I came to a wide open space. I knew this field. It had shown up in my mind after Nanny Alice passed.

I followed my instinct and knew that this field was home for me, a new space to meet Spirit.

Before a show or a reading, I picture myself on this road, walking barefoot on the packed dirt. It's soft like clay. I approach the field. The grass is plush under my feet, I can feel the sun on my face and positive energy is swirling all around me. I stand there, ready for Spirit.

This is a sacred space for me. No one else comes into this field except Spirit. This field changes and evolves each time I visit. Once, while I was writing my mother's eulogy, a boulder-sized rock showed up, a clear reflection of my mental status at the time. I was stuck, and couldn't put the words together.

Once I was done with the eulogy and had delivered it, the rock disappeared. Something had shifted inside me. I found my peace. Now, when I head to the field before a reading, if it's clear, I know that I am okay. I am prepared. And I am ready.

Jennie's Gems

WHAT YOU PUT INTO YOUR LIFE HAS A FAR GREATER RETURN ON INVESTMENT THAN ANY BANK ACCOUNT.

The Emotional Junk Drawer

Every home has at least one junk drawer. It's the spot for things you don't know what to do with, things you might have to use one day, and a variety of bad choices: stupid things you bought, crap you can't let go of, objects you can't even identify. If you needed any of these items, they'd have a proper place, right?

So the question I want to ask is not whether you have a junk drawer, but how many you have. In your house and in your mind.

The junk drawer is a mirror to the emotions we are holding on to. For whatever reason, you need to pack away your feelings for future use. Sometimes, you can't even remember the last time you needed to drag your morose ass out of the house. You are holding on to all the old shit in your emotional junk drawer. All the things you might need—excuses, anger, resentment— are the things you need to get rid of. Why the fuck would you want to keep that shit? None of that serves you, but you're hanging onto it, just in case. Why are you dealing yourself a hand of fucked-up-edness?

I know it's hard to move on when you don't know where to start. Let me help you out with this exercise.

Empty one of your literal junk drawers. Dump it into a bag or a box and place the contents somewhere out of reach (out of sight, out of mind really works).

Hide it in the garage or the basement or the shed. Take note of how this makes you feel. Probably a little anxious and confused. Pack those feelings away with the other, tangible, shit.

Tell everyone in your household that the drawer needs to remain empty for at least a month. If they need something from that drawer, by all means, go find the box/bag and get what they need. Or find the spot where that junk was supposed to live in the first place. If you had pens and notepads in your kitchen junk drawer, there's a good chance you already have those items in a home office or your handbag.

By the end of that month, you can fill that drawer again, but not with junk. Fill it with something that serves you. Maybe it's the art supplies you always want to use but that are tucked away in the basement. Maybe it's a spot of honour for your favourite cooking utensils that always get clumped in with the dollar-store spatulas. The point of this exercise is to help you realize that when you empty your junk drawer, you make space for the things you value and the things that have meaning. That's what will help you move forward. When you reach into that drawer for something you feel you need, look into the empty drawer and find something else in your personal inventory that can help you. Let go of the crap from the past.

The Garden of Grief

I'm not much of a gardener myself, but I sure can appreciate the work that goes into a beautiful garden. I can take just as much pleasure in a garden of natural chaos as I can in one that is perfectly planned. Wildflowers are just as pretty as rose bushes. Dandelions provide food for the bees. Peonies, with their fluttering, imperfect petals, are just a wonderfully happy flower.

Because they are perennials, peonies will come back year after year, but they're never quite the same. One year, the blossoms may emerge later or the blooms might be smaller. That is the nature of the natural world. Grief works the same way.

I want you to be okay with your grief manifesting differently year after year. In fact, it can change month to month or day to day. That's normal. You are not leaving the memory of your loved one behind if you have a good day. You *can* enjoy your life. You *can* be happy.

Grief is such a deep-rooted emotion that it is impossible to bury or ignore it. It comes in waves for most people. Grief can be triggered by completely unrelated events. I've seen people completely lose their shit four years after a loved one has passed when they eat a bowl of popcorn.

Listen, I'm never going to tell you to "get over it." I

just don't want you to be stuck in your grief. Make the choice to coexist with the permanent loss. When grief punches you in the face, say thank you, because you are still alive to feel something. Your garden will continue to grow if you let it, even if everything has changed.

The Back Burner

Without question, nearly all of us prefer to use right front burner. It has the easiest access and is in the right place for a right-handed world. It doesn't even have to be the biggest or best-burning element, because we will still prefer to use it.

The right front burner is perfect for quickly sautéing vegetables and cooking bacon. It's where the action is. It's how dinner gets made. Everything else— the canned corn, the frozen peas, the slow-simmering stock—gets put on the back burner.

The exception is for those of us living in a shitty rental where only three of the burners work at all and the precious right front burner scorches anything that you dare cook on it. And that's a metaphor all on its own.

Oof. Can there be a more relevant analogy for life? What the fuck are you putting on your back burner? And why is it still sitting there? It could boil over at any second and fuck up your whole kitchen with that terrible burnt corn smell.

What is boiling over in your soul that you are not giving yourself permission to attend to?

All the ingredients have equal value, you know. The corn is as important for your stir fry as the onions and garlic cooking on the front.

What's on the front burner of your life? Probably your job, your kids, and your finances. The responsibilities. If you're like most people, the things we put on the back burner are the things we truly desire. Our art. Our creativity. Our true purpose.

I did it too, when I was working an office job and not setting myself free to be the medium I truly am. I put that on the back burner. But when I changed places, when I moved the boring day job to the back and turned the heat high on mediumship, a funny thing happened. I *thrived*! I was no longer content to let my true self simmer in the back. Like a pot of cold water, I had to be patient. It took time for my new career to come to a full boil.

People can encourage us or shit all over us and we sometimes still won't move the dream from the back burner. It gives us a reason for doubt, or to make excuses. We already know what needs to be brought to the front in our lives, but we shove it to the back, where it doesn't require attention. If it's not critically important at that moment, we feel we have enough time to negotiate. Don't let your dreams simmer unattended.

Your North Star

What is your North Star?

Unlike all the other stars in the sky, the North Star, also known as Polaris, is in the same location every night.

For me, the North Star is a metaphor for keeping on track with a personal mission statement. It's a fixed destination that you can depend on in your life as the world changes around you. From anywhere in the northern hemisphere, the North Star will show you where true north is. It's a guiding light that can help you make the other big decisions in your life.

Once you decide what your personal North Star is, figure out what your commitment is to it. Your knees might still be shaky when you find your mission, but trust me, your legs will hold you up. Your conviction will give you strength. Your passion has a backbone.

Grief is a good place to start from in your search for a mission statement. When life takes something significant away from you, you are forced to wake up. In your darkest day, you can call on your North Star to show up for you and help you move forward. Keep your focus on your purpose and it will help you pull yourself out of grief.

Coming Out and Stepping In

I needed to come out in order to come into who I really was. I couldn't have one without the other. When I chose to come out, I got rid of all the junk of others, of loves that weren't right for me. I turned the page, and opened up my world to fresh new opportunities.

I was 28 years old, I was dating a hypnotist (male), and selling sex toys at home parties. I was killing it. Still, I was feeling there had to be more to life. I wasn't feeling any connection to the men I was dating.

I had a slow realization that when I was with a woman, I didn't feel like I was just there to fulfil her sexual desires, like I did when I was with a man. I felt more present and available. I pushed my feelings aside, though, because my mom was gay and to me, being a lesbian looked like abuse and dysfunction. I *did not* want that and I didn't want to be anything like my mother, so I forced myself into relationships with men.

When I acknowledged who I really was, I stopped caring what other people thought. That was my biggest lesson from coming out. I had to be okay with myself in order to find happiness. I had to come out to come into the true story of myself.

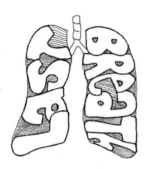

The Last Breath

Having read more than 17,000 people, I can say with certainty that guilt and grief tend to look the same. It's typical to feel a hole in your heart for not being there when your loved one took their last breath. That can be guilt over your absence or grief over the loss. It's hard to separate the two.

Nobody ever dies alone. We've been taught we need to rush and drop everything to be there to watch the body physically die, but it's not true. There is nothing comforting in watching a loved one take their last choking breath or piss themselves or see life drain out. Truthfully, by the time death arrives, they are already in transition. They are ready to move on. They are feeling the pull of Spirit. They are already trying on new shoes.

I often think of Alzheimer's and dementia patients as a good example of how our Spirit leaves before we die. They walk that line between here and there, fluctuating between this world and the Spirit world.

The process of death can take *fucking forever*, but the actual dying part is one second. Physical death takes time and is not the same as Spiritual passing. Our bodies are here in the physical world until we die, then our Spirit moves on. Life changes, but it doesn't end.

Energy never dies. Its fluidity makes our Spirit life continuous.

Death is out of our control. It will come for all of us, but we don't know when. In my shows, I am always telling people to seize the crap out of life. Do your best with the time you are given. Make smart choices.

One of the most memorable readings for me was that of a 39-year-old mom with three kids under 12. She was dying from an incurable disease. During an end-of-life visit I had with her, she wondered why the good people die first and the bastards never die.

"I wish I could change bodies just so I could physically be here to watch my kids grow up," she said.

But we can't do that. What we can do is get moving. Shovel away the garbage that is no longer serving you. Yeah, it's going to take a whole lot of fucking courage to make a big change.

I challenge you to write your eulogy, right here, right now. What do you want people to remember about you? What is your legacy? What are your victories?

If you can't list them, you aren't living them. Think deep and hard about what is standing in your way. Take your first steps on the journey to get closer to your purpose and passion. It's not good enough to wait around to die.

Stop protesting the shit that doesn't matter. Connect to your soul, to what you really crave and desire. Learn to shut up and listen. It's there, in the whisper of Spirit—the one within you—where you'll find your happiness.

YOU-LOGY

I t's fitting that I close this book out with my own You-logy. After all, when we are the authors of our own eulogies we can control the conversation. So here goes.

I had no hand in deciding to be present—physically, anyways—in this life. But I sure as hell decided that while I was here, I would live large, eat donairs, and be wholly and authentically me without permission from others. There will never be another me in the physical world, but my energy will stick around to be part of you.

I honestly do not want any of you to miss me just because I am not in the physical body that you have so grown to love. That 5-foot-10, energy bigger than the space I took up, foul-mouthed, rocked the boat, didn't give a shit about what others thought, saggy big-boobed with a spare tire that would make the Michelin man jealous body.

You're here because you want to save space for honouring me. What I'd rather you do today is sit back, grab a drink or a pickle, and remember what you learned from me. Please make sure it's nice. Then go and get a tattoo of my full face on your body. Okay, that may be a bit of a big ask. Please don't get lost in grief because I am no longer here. Scream out the grief until your throat is sore then please move the fuck on. You won't find me in grief.

I tried to embrace the conventional way of living. Wait, that's a lie. I never embraced the conventional way of living, I just welcomed experiences and the gifts they brought into my life. Life was like a treasure hunt to me. I listened to where I was being led even though it was not always rainbows and butterflies. I was to follow that path for a reason and it was up to me to explore why. When I did, I'd find another clue, an answer, or the secret to the meaning of life. Okay, that's a lie, too. It's not a secret: the meaning of life is to discover who you are and be that fantastic person for the rest of your time on Earth.

You are all here to celebrate the experience that we had together because we chose to experience a piece of our lives together. And for that I say thank you. Remember to always make sure that your emotional doorbell works so that when I come and haunt your ass, you can answer the goddamn door. Show up or fuck off.

Slap this on your do-now list, so that you can keep hanging out with me: Create a space where you can feel my energy. Whether that is a field, by a river, thinking of me while you are waiting in line at the drive-thru, or a memory of us sitting in one of the favourite spots where we had an experience together. Then, when you are fully present and can feel my energy, let's hang out. And don't think for a minute that if I ruffled feathers in your life, that it will be any different now that I'm in Spirit world.

Find me in our experiences that meant something to you. Find me in the quietness of your mind and let your mind wander. Find me when you are feeling on top of the world, in the lowest moment of your life, or even in the middle of nowhere. I'm the one wearing yellow rain boots and sitting under a palm tree.

And that smell? That wasn't me.

Acknowledgments

Dana Goldstein, talented ghostwriter and producer wth patience galore. What a journey we have had together between filming a pilot for TV and this book. Epsom salts were required.

The talented editing team: Zoey Duncan and Catherine Szabo. You made things make more sense.

My daughter Shelby who inspires me every day to do better and be better. I love you more than much.

Thank you Andrea and Anthony Northey for giving me many new beginnings in my life. Thank you for truly being my cheerleaders.

Amy Bishop, talented illustrator for this book and a grounded support in my life.

My cousin Michelle Ogilvie who untiringly searches for my birth father, and who has been by my side for all days. I love you.

My best friend of over 20 years, Susan Saunders, who has supported this crazy journey of mine.

My mother, Carolyn Ogilvie. March 1949 - April 2021. Rest peacefully.

My grandmother, Alice Ogilvie, my greatest inspiration and beacon of light.

To my high school teachers: Linda Wheaton and Helen Seymour. Thank you for caring more than you needed to.

About the Author

Jennie Ogilvie is one of Canada's favourite mediums. While based in Calgary, Alberta, Jennie's shows sell out from coast-to-coast. To learn more, buy an event ticket, or book a private or group session, visit her website JennieOgilvie.com.

Manufactured by Amazon.ca
Bolton, ON

40760090R00146